Other Books by
Elliott S. Dacher, M.D.

Aware, Awake, Alive

Integral Health

Intentional Healing

Whole Healing

D1565649

Transitions

A Guide to the 6 Stages
of a Successful Life Transition

ELLIOTT S. DACHER, M.D.

WISDOM PRESS
New York, NY

The information and advice contained in this book are based upon the research and the personal and professional experiences of the author. They are not intended as a substitute for consulting with a healthcare professional. The author is not responsible for any adverse effects or consequences resulting from the use of any of the suggestions, preparations, or procedures discussed in this book. All matters pertaining to your physical health should be supervised by a healthcare professional.

Wisdom Press
New York, NY
www.elliottdacher.org

Excerpt from "The Road Not Taken" from the book THE POETRY OF ROBERT FROST edited by Edward Connery Lathem. Copyright © 1916, 1969 by Henry Holt and Company, copyright © 1944 by Robert Frost. Reprinted by arrangement with Henry Holt and Company, LLC. All rights reserved.

Excerpt from "Love After Love" from THE POETRY OF DEREK WALCOTT 1948–2013 by Derek Walcott, selected by Glyn Maxwell. Copyright © 2014 by Derek Walcott. Reprinted by permission of Farrar, Straus and Giroux, LLC.

The lines from "November 1968". Copyright © 1993 by Adrienne Rich. Copyright © 1971 by W. W. Norton & Company, Inc, from COLLECTED EARLY POEMS: 1950–1970 by Adrienne Rich. Used by permission of W. W. Norton & Company, Inc.

ISBN: 978-0-9836371-2-7

Copyright © 2016 by Elliott S. Dacher, M.D.

All rights reserved. No part of this publication may be reproduced, stored in a retrieval system, or transmitted, in any form or by any means, electronic, mechanical, photocopying, recording, or otherwise, without the prior written permission of the copyright owner.

INTERIOR AND COVER DESIGN: Gary A. Rosenberg
EDITOR: Carol Killman Rosenberg

Printed in the United States of America

For You and All Others
Who Summon Forth the Courage
Through Challenge and Adversity
To Reach for a Larger Life and Health
By Virtue of Your Journey
May You Discover and Live a Precious Human Life

Contents

A Letter to My Reader ix

1. Shape Shifting 1
   Our lives can take two paths: automaticity or consciousness.
   In the first instance, we ignore the call to change. In the second
   instance, we accept the call and learn how to reshape our lives.

● ● ●

2. STAGE ONE: The Call to a Larger Life 13
   In each of our lives there are moments of unexpected adversity
   that summon us to reconsider the direction of our lives. These
   moments are the soul's call for change.

3. STAGE TWO: The Departure 39
   When we set out on the journey of transition, we leave behind
   our old ways of living. As we move from outdated ways to a
   revitalized life, we must let go of those beliefs and habitual
   patterns that will not serve future growth.

4. STAGE THREE: The In-Between Time 53
   When our past slowly drifts into our rearview mirror and
   our future is still undefined, we enter an in-between time that
   separates our previous life from our yet-to-be future. This is a
   difficult time of exploration, reflection, and, finally, transformation.

5. STAGE FOUR: Lessons Learned 69
   There are many lessons that are learned as we traverse the
   in-between time. This is a different kind of education than we
   are accustomed to. We learn about humility, impermanence,
   interconnectedness, trust, and living in the present moment.
   We learn how to live with authenticity and passionate aliveness.

6. STAGE FIVE: **The Return**............................87
When the in-between time is over, we return to day-to-day life.
We establish new values, reshape our sense of self, and adopt
new lifestyles, and we share with others the knowledge
and wisdom gained through our journey.

7. STAGE SIX: **The Gold**............................105
The rewards of transition and conscious living are joy, peace,
love, and freedom. However, these are not as we previously
knew them. They are profound, sustained, resilient,
trustworthy, and inner-based.

● ● ●

8. **A Healthy Human Life and Beyond**......................119
For those who wish to journey to the far reaches of human
potential, there is still more. Beyond a healthy human life
that emerges from our transitions is the profound experience
of oneness. This arrives at the highest level of consciousness:
unity consciousness. It brings an end to separateness and
conveys unique and extended human capacities.

Afterword...127

Working with Elliott: Personal Mentoring 129

Suggested Readings 131

Retreat Facilities...................................135

A Letter to My Reader

Not in his goals but in his transitions man is great.

—RALPH WALDO EMERSON

There are times in each of our lives when our well-ordered existence seems to crack open, and life no longer seems to work as it once did. This may occur slowly over time or with an unexpected suddenness. We may be taken over by a persistent boredom and discontent, or feel the subtle sense that something is just not right. We may be shocked by an unexpected loss, disabling emotional distress, or physical disease. Or perhaps we may have simply reached the time in life when we can no longer avoid the inner longing that knows that there is something more—something more meaningful and more possible for our life.

When our old life structure begins to come apart, we are at the entranceway to a life transition, a very special, sacred, and pregnant time that is filled with unseen and well-disguised possibilities. If this opportunity is taken up and fully lived and experienced, our lives will expand and we will be reborn into a larger well-being full of new possibilities. But if we refuse or deny this opportunity, our life will stagnate, accompanied by the signs and symptoms of persistent emotional distress and potentially premature illness, whose source will seem obscure to ordinary vision.

And so it is that we find ourselves confronting the great transitions in our life at moments of pain, distress, and disease. At such times, we most acutely feel fear, disorientation, and the unknown. Reaching outside for help, we may consult a psychologist or physician, hoping for a remedy to our distress. And at times there is help—temporary relief from physical suffering, new psychological tools, and maybe even a "cure."

What we call "ordinary" health may return, and that is good. But if that is all that happens, it is a false achievement. Unfortunately most psychologists and physicians are not trained to see or cultivate the all important life transition that is the hidden message and possibility embedded in our distress. We may feel better, but the opportunity to be reborn into a revitalized life and health may well be lost to the narrowness and blindness of a limited view of health, healing, and human possibility.

So, to grasp this opportunity, we must look beyond the limited training of our usual helpers, see through the darkness, accept the call to a new life, fall in love with the possibilities, and find inspiration in the great stories of transition and change. We can learn from the journey of Odysseus, the quest of Parsifal, the trials of Job, Joseph Campbell's *Hero of a Thousand Faces,* or perhaps our next-door neighbor. These great stories offer us a map that can guide us through the confusion and darkness, reconnect us to our soul, and bring forth the light of a larger life. It is a map that provides us with a clear picture of the stages and process of transition, a map that can help us transform suffering, pain, and disease into the great human treasures of wholeness, peace, love, and joy. It is this map that I will begin to share with you here.

My first opportunity to share my experience with a larger audience occurred when I began writing a health column for a local newspaper many years ago. One of my first columns, entitled "Transitions," got an unexpected and somewhat surprising response. People called me at my medical office and stopped me on the street, asking, "How did you know what I've been living through?" After we shared a few words, they would thank me and then add, "I thought there was something wrong with me. I felt so alone." The tone of their voices and the look in their eyes indicated relief—they were relieved to know that someone else understood and that they were not alone or "crazy."

It is difficult enough to transform one's life. And when we do, it often seems as though we have no choice but to do it through trial and error. However, the sequential stages of a life transition have been known for millennia. In very personal and passionate terms, those who went before us left us a roadmap written in poetry and prose. The guidance they offered provides precise details, illuminates the path, reassures the soul, and assists with a safe passage. So we are fortunate to have their knowledge. It is like we have found a friend, mentor, and fellow traveler in our wise ancestors who took the road less traveled. In the pages that follow, my intention is to explore with you this age-old knowledge.

There are six stages of a life transition: *The Call, The Departure, The In-Between Time, Lessons Learned, The Return,* and *The Gold.* The call from our depths, the first stage of a life transition, arrives in many ways. It may follow an unexpected loss, persistent mental stress or distress, the onset of physical disease, the aging process, or a more subtly quiet yet persistent sense that there is "more to life." Our distress calls us to personal renewal.

There are times when this call slowly builds over years. There are other times when we begin to lose control as the pillars of our well-ordered life rapidly fall apart. In either instance, we are at the entranceway to a life transition, a very special, sacred, and pregnant time filled with unseen possibilities. When the call comes, we each have a choice. We can refuse it through denial, procrastination, distraction, or grasping at numbing transient pleasures. To do so turns our life back to what was, to the outdated habits and patterns of the past. We invite both stagnation and spiritual decay—losing personal power, creativity, and vitality—a loss that shows up years later as persistent emotional distress and premature disease.

This critical period, when we hear and are summoned to answer the call to change, is a momentous time of our life. If we answer the call, it is a time when the courage and risks taken will determine, for years to come, the character of our lives. Those who choose to accept the call and pass through the threshold will enter the second stage of transition.

The departure is the second stage of transition. The poet T. S. Eliot wrote, "The end is where we start from." Endings are a dying off and separation from certain parts of our life that no longer work for us. This may include relationships, lifestyles, work, meanings, or the false sense of immortality. This second stage is difficult. It can be filled with disenchantment and disillusionment, which accompanies a painful recognition that what was once our life will no longer work and cannot be fixed. There are a mixture of feelings—loss, sadness, aloneness, emotional pain, fear, relief, excitement, and the anticipation of adventure. One or more of these feelings may dominate your experience.

Having separated from aspects of your previous life and identity, a process that may take months or longer, we next enter the in-between time, the third stage of transition. That's a special time—one could say, a sacred time—that separates past from future. It is like a "parenthesis" in our life, a time of reflection, contemplation, simple being, and spontaneous discovery, often mixed with anxiety and fear. It is during the in-between time that we gain new insights into our life, learning what we need to know in order to move forward. The in-between time may last for months or longer. It is a difficult, yet wonderful, time. There are moments of great joy and moments of suffering, times of great insight and times that seem boring and useless. But all the time, a new life is incubating.

We learn many lessons during the in-between time, lessons that will guide the return to a new life. That is the fourth stage of transition. We learn about humility, impermanence, living in the present moment, listening to our deeper self, trusting inner wisdom, and living in accord with our true nature. These lessons do not arrive all at once. They emerge as we allow an open space for insight and wisdom to arise from our depths. Each lesson learned becomes our own. It is not inherited from family or culture. It's our wisdom, our knowledge, our nature. It's the only basis for an authentic life.

After the necessary time of incubation and self-discovery, renewed and revitalized, we are ready to take the first tentative steps toward integrating our newfound truths into day-to-day life. The return is the fifth stage of transition. It is a time of trying out new values, beliefs, identities, and lifestyles, while at all times holding our authentic center. The return is at first a tender and vulnerable time. Over time, we accommodate to our new life, progressively feeling a previously unknown sense of authenticity, confidence, balance, and harmony.

As a result of the courage to undertake transition, we progressively gain the fruits of this journey. The reward for the completion of this heroic adventure is the return home to who and what we are: the return home to health and healing of mind, body, and spirit, the return home to a renewed life of authenticity, joy, and freedom. Stripped of old fears, limitations, illusions, and fantasies, we can engage life with the freshness of an early spring morning. Briefly at first, and then more assuredly, we experience an authentic happiness and peace, wisdom, and freedom. These are not given from the outside. They are gained on the inside through the efforts of our life transition. Not dependent on outside circumstances, they are hardy, resistant, and immune to the difficulties and adversities of life. That is the sixth stage of transition, the Gold.

These are the six stages of a life transition. As difficult and as treacherous as it may seem, when the ripening occurs and a revitalized life begins to return, you come to know that the modern-day hero no longer fights his battles on the fields of Troy or the beaches of Normandy, but rather plants his flag on the battlefield of the soul. And the peace and healing we find inside becomes the peace that will be found outside. Through our own courage to engage change, we become an inspiration to others, the seed for a better world.

You may ask, "Why do I have to go through this while others seem to be happy and never in crisis?" Perhaps it is no more complex than the realization that some of us are born to be seekers and some not, and some of us are destined for a larger healing and wholing, and others not. In *The Diary of Anaïs Nin,* Volume 6 1955–1956, the writer Anaïs Nin stated it this way:

> I live the personal drama responsible for the larger one, seeking a cure. Perhaps it is the greater agony to live this life in which my awareness makes a thousand revolutions while others make only one. My span may seem smaller but it is really larger because it covers all the obscure routes of the soul and body, never receiving medals for its courage.

You may further inquire as to what all of this has to do with health and healing? Why would a physician trained as a healer write about transition and transformation? Years of medical practice have taught me how easy it is to close the door on the valuable teaching moments of distress and disease, precious moments that contain the possibility of personal transformation. That rare opportunity to gain a larger life, a door that may open only a few times in a lifetime, is too often and too quickly closed with diagnostic labels, drugs, and treatments. This is not to disparage the importance of modern medicine, However, it is to point out that treatment devoid of a larger view of healing deprives us of the opportunity to go beyond remedies to the deeper transformation and healing we are called to by distress and disease. Transition and transformation are at the core of a vital and ongoing healing process.

To successfully traverse a life transition requires personal heroism, a willingness to question, to risk, let go of the past, and adventure into the unknown. In ancient times, cultures provided rituals, practices, and guidance that assisted individuals in responding to life's changes. But, in our time, these ancient guides and rituals are all gone. We feel as if we are left alone. That is why we need to understand the six stages of transition shared by those who preceded us. Without that knowledge, we are limited to trial and error, and the entire outcome remains in question.

"It must be fully understood," said the famed psychologist C. G. Jung in *Modern Man in Search of a Soul*, "that the mere fact of living in the present does not make a man modern, for in that case everyone presently alive would be so. He alone is modern who is fully conscious of the present. . . . Indeed, he is completely modern only when he has come to the very edge of the world, leaving behind him all that has been discarded and outgrown, and acknowledging that he stands before a void out of which all things may grow."

This book began in that void. It began at the time of my first major transition. It is not meant to be merely informative. It is meant to be a companion and guide on your journey through a life transition. To know that you are not alone is helpful and reassuring. To understand the process assures you that you are quite sane at the difficult moments you may question it. To know what is ahead can save you the detours that come with trial and error. This book is meant to serve those purposes and come alive as you courageously pursue the transitions in your life.

If we can accomplish this task, in Joseph Campbell's words in *The Hero with a Thousand Faces*, "Where we thought to find an abomination, we shall find a god; where we had thought to slay another, we shall slay ourselves; where we had thought to travel outward, we shall come to the center of our existence; where we had thought to be alone, we shall be with all the world."

In the pages that follow, I will ask you to use your transitions, not squander them.

Chapter 1

Shape Shifting

Long have you timidly waded, holding a plank by the shore,
Now I will you to be a bold swimmer,
To jump off in the midst of the sea, and rise again and nod to me
and shout, and laughingly dash with your hair.
—WALT WHITMAN, FROM "SONG OF MYSELF"

Transitions are wonderfully troublesome times. They are as necessary for the survival and growth of soul and spirit as water and food are for physical development. The awakening of consciousness is as essential to human development as is biological evolution. Although life transitions rarely come at convenient times, they always come at the right time. They arrive to rescue us from a part of our life that has been lived to completion and deliver us to an aspect of life that is yet unknown. When we succeed in our transitions, we shift the shape of our future life.

There was once a time when community and culture carefully conveyed to the individual—through ceremony, rituals, and rites of passage—the understandings and practices of the major life transitions: youth to adulthood to elderhood. That cultural process assured smooth and predictable transition that were in accord with the framework of a given society. The individual's life, from birth to death and beyond, was culturally and communally defined. The great transitions of life were structured and ordered. Questions such as "Who am I?" and "What is my life about?" bore no relevance. But that ancient world, with both its advantages and limitations, is no longer available to modern men and women.

We are no longer the predestined product of culturally determined roles, identities, and social customs. The center of gravity has shifted from community to individual, from ritual and social formulas to the self-developing, self-determining, self-realizing individual of modern times. We are released from the boundaries of social conditioning, social structures, and the guidance of a narrowly focused community. But released into what? For us, the questions "Who am I?" and "What is my life about?" are of great importance and as well a source of great difficulty. These are the essential questions to be asked and solved by modern men and women in the midst of the inner and outer challenges of day-to-day life.

There are two fundamental responses to this unique circumstance of modern times. The first is to fail to ask either question. In this instance, we succumb to a life that is largely set in place by the idiosyncrasies of parenting, early education, and cultural values. Such lives, more or less, run on automatic from beginning to end. For these individuals, a healthy life may be possible, but a fully awakened and experienced life is not. However, if we are truly fortunate, we can summon forth the inspiration, initiative, and courage to respond to life's challenges by taking these questions as an ongoing process of self-discovery and self-evolution.

In the first instance, we have the example of Willy Loman, the tragic figure in Arthur Miller's *Death of a Salesman*. In the character of Willy, Miller offers us a window into a modern-day life lived on automatic. Willy cannot understand, respond to, or grow into loss, aging, or the shifting circumstances of his life. Today and tomorrow are another version of yesterday. Personal growth is stunted. Adversity is met with denial, defensiveness, and reactivity. Thoreau called such lives ones of "quiet desperation." Joseph

Campbell similarly referred to them as desperate circumstances. Lacking the capacity to expand consciousness and the scope of life, such individuals wander through their days, from beginning to end, unaware of their dilemma. From the perspective of what is possible, they have squandered their lives.

Compare this to the hero stories of earlier Western literature, the stories of coming to consciousness, the stories of awakening. Whether it be the release from the enslavement in Plato's *Allegory of the Cave,* the journey of *Odysseus,* Parsifal's search for the Holy Grail, the Journey of Oedipus from king to pauper to wise man, or Campbell's *Hero of a Thousand Faces,* we discover the character and courage of the self-determining, self-realizing individual—one who chooses personal evolution to stagnation. We see in these stories the sequential stages of transition traversed by the modern hero, and the great "boon," as Campbell refers to it that is the fruit of this inspired and impassioned effort.

Modern individuals confront these tipping points at times of distress and suffering. They are our pivot points in modern times. They are the critical moments in which we either step up to a larger life or fall back into the old and familiar. How we relate to adversity defines the life that follows. Do we choose denial, outdated perspectives, ineffectual habituated patterns, and well-worn reactions (all of which are unconscious to the individual), or do we see adversity, distress, and suffering as gateways to a larger, awakened life?

Two Paths: Automaticity and Consciousness

Our lives generally follow one of two built-in blueprints: *conditioned automaticity* or *awakened consciousness.* The first is composed of a large group of programmed psychological perspectives and responses imprinted in our psyche early in life. They perpetuate the attitudes and styles of family and culture. This is a conservative system that seeks to maintain the status quo. It is rarely questioned. It relies on fixed ways of perceiving the world and equally fixed habitual response patterns. These fixed patterns of perception and reaction define the character of such a life.

We all know how this works. We interpret our life experience in familiar ways and respond with equally familiar reactions. Circumstances may change, but we perceive and mentally shape them to accommodate our learned and fixed templates. The default mechanism is automaticity. We wonder why we always end up in the same situation, why things just never seem to change. But there is not enough curiosity or initiative to examine the workings of the conditioned mind.

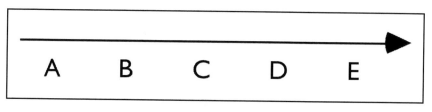

FIGURE 1. Automaticity

Point "A" on Figure 1 represents the pattern of automaticity whose sources are the perceptual and psychological patterns learned early in life. Once established, these patterns direct our lives in a straight line. However, our lives will invariably have their "bumps" (B through E above), challenges to the normal flow of life. These disruptive moments may be initiated by illness, loss, excessive stress, aging, unsatisfying success, or the disappointments associated with failure. As indicated by the arrow, irrespective of these potentially life-transforming challenges, life remains much the same. And most often, at the midpoint of an automated life, there is a downward drift of stagnation as life reaches its end point, devoid of the vitality and adaptability of a conscious life.

If we follow the path of an automated life, there is little flexibility in dealing with life's challenges. There are only two possible responses: *denial* and *procrastination*. Either of these responses assures the continuity of an automated life. They maintain the status quo. In the first instance, we deny the existence of distress by unconsciously blocking unpleasant experiences, by avoiding or withdrawing from distress, occupying ourselves with one distraction or another, or treating distress with self-betraying transient pleasures. In the second instance, we simply wait and bear the problem at hand, perhaps trying one remedy or another, always hoping the difficulty at hand will pass by itself. In each instance, our response and its consequences are largely unconscious.

Denial and procrastination offer us a quick, though illusionary, reprieve from the normal and inevitable adversities of life. We are relieved of the necessity to examine, question, and, if required, change our lives. Life's transitional moments will invariably be lost, and there will arise an increasing discord between how we live our life and the deeper calling of our soul. Most often this resistance to life's natural flow and call for change shows up as a physical or emotional symptom. It is then labeled and treated by a professional with drugs of one sort or another, while its deeper source is unseen and ignored.

The second possibility, a more recent one in human existence, results from the development of the prefrontal cortex and the simultaneous emergence and evolution of human consciousness. This allows for moment-to-moment innovation, flexibility, attention to the unique circumstance of each moment, and self-inquiry. An evolving consciousness perceives and responds to life in accordance with the freshness of the moment and the actuality of the circumstance as it is. It is uninfluenced by preexisting perceptual and reaction patterns. An awakened consciousness must be chosen and cultivated. It is neither passed on at birth, nor given to us by family or culture. It emerges and matures through inner development. It is the sign of an evolved and dynamic life that utilizes the conscious capacities that have developed in the modern evolution of the human brain.

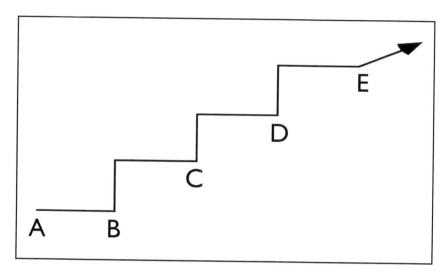

FIGURE 2. The Conscious Life

Figure 2 depicts the second path that life may take, the path of a shape shifter, the path of an awakening consciousness. As in Figure 1, it begins at point "A" where our familial and cultural conditioning defines and shapes our life, pointing it in a straight and unchanging direction. Yet, when distress and disruption occur (B through E), when life seems to stop for a moment and a crack suddenly appears in the automated routine of daily life, these individuals do not reach out for a remedy to anesthetize the tension, pain, and suffering that invariably accompanies these moments. There is no grasping at money, power, possessions, treatments, drugs, or dependent relationships. There is no denial or procrastination. Such individuals learn to love the question, "Why me and why now?"

These individuals see adversity as an opportunity to reconsider and reshape their lives. Adversity becomes a precious teacher of life. They invest in growth and development rather than the status quo. They seek a more conscious and vital life. Values, lifestyles, attitudes, and social relationships are open to reconsideration. They are available and eager to engage the stages of a life transition. The vertical lines in Figure 2 represent the transitional process initiated by the life events (B–E). Once the transitional process, the vertical leap, has brought forth a new structure and direction, there is a period of time, often lasting many years (the horizontal lines), during which these individuals fully develop the potential unleashed by the growth in consciousness that accompanied the transition process.

There is a leap in consciousness, capacity, resourcefulness, vitality, and authenticity, a growth in attention, mindfulness, and presence in life. We become increasingly free to be as we are, unchained from our past, and living in the naked truth of the moment. The light of awareness, stripped of the past, illuminates the nowness of each moment. Although the insights of an awakening consciousness may come as a sudden "aha," there is a progressive process of incremental growth of personal freedom that underlies these sudden breakthroughs. All of this is aborted if we fall back into an automated life, failing to navigate life's transitions.

However, this is not an all-or-nothing situation. Our lives are a mixture of automated and conscious living. Individuals who live automated lives do change and grow. They develop careers, invest in relationships, and nurture families. They are often good people living decent lives. Their growth, however, is always restrained, and their possibilities are similarly limited. It is a life, but a limited one.

One never knows when a life that runs on automatic may undergo a radical shift toward transition and change. I've been fooled too many times. As a result, I've learned to respect and hold in awe the mystery of life and its unfolding, and how love, a particular person, an unexpected revelation, or a life-threatening disease can alter the course of a life that previously followed a straight line. Because we never know, we can never pass judgment on the character, rhythm, or pace of the unfolding of another's life.

Once experienced, future transitions lose much of their fearfulness and uncertainty. What was previously looked at with apprehension and fear can now be approached with interest and anticipation. We've learned to focus our attention, let go of unnecessary activities, allow for more solitude, and carefully listen to what is moving in our lives. Care, patience, sensitivity, and discerning action will allow us to move through change with greater ease. We master the skill of shape shifting—the skill of consciously reshaping our lives by successfully traversing life's transitions, big and small. We have learned the art of shape shifting.

Overcoming

There is an evolutionary impulse in each of us, in life itself. That is how life has evolved from the smallest life form to the complex human experience. We can experience that impulse as a nagging sense that there is more to life, a frustration with our limitations, boredom, or an inner restlessness. We may experience as a deep longing or yearning to know life at its fullest. If we nurture this impulse, it will grow and save our life, culture, and planet. It will allow for the continued growth of life toward its final maturity. That is why, as Emerson said, there is greatness in our transitions.

The philosopher Friedrich Nietzsche, in his book *Thus Spake Zarathustra,* states that it is man's task to overcome man. This seeming paradox expresses a transcendent understanding of humankind's life journey, an understanding that has been restated over and over by wise men and women. Nietzsche was speaking about the conscious man overcoming the automatic man.

The German poet Rainer Rilke states it another way. He says

that at birth we are all given a sealed envelope that contains the mystery of life. Some of us are meant to open the envelope and live conscious lives, while others seem destined to leave the envelope unopened, living a more or less automatic life, and passing the unopened envelope to the next generation.

In *Psychology and Religion Volume 11: West and East,* the psychologist C. G. Jung offers a further perspective on overcoming:

> The difference between the "natural" individuation process, which runs its course unconsciously, and the one which is consciously realized, is tremendous. In the first case consciousness nowhere intervenes; the end remains as dark as the beginning. In the second case so much darkness comes to light that the personality is permeated with light, and consciousness necessarily gains in scope and insight.

Each one of us will, out of necessity, confront events that disrupt our lives. They invariably urge us toward change. Our only choice lies in deciding what we do with these challenges. Do we maintain a fixed and unchanging life, living on automatic, or do we step up to a life based on an awakening consciousness? Do we choose to carry the outdated past into the future, or do we discover a larger life permeated with light? The choice is ours. And that choice will determine the character and fate of our one precious lifetime.

HEART ADVICE FROM A FELLOW TRAVELER

1. I am certain that what enabled me to move through my first major transition was the knowledge and inspiration acquired from others who had gone before and left a precise roadmap for others to follow.

Although I knew that the passage could only be done alone,

in a sense I never felt alone. I always felt the presence of the great myths and stories, of yesterday's life explorers.

At the most difficult moments, I was able to take stock of my situation and compare it to these roadmaps to see if I was going in the correct direction. When I craved solitude and time alone, I wanted to be certain I was not withdrawing or pushing people away, but rather doing the positive work of transition. When I questioned my sanity, it was of great value to know that others had taken this road before me and that they were quite sane. When I ran into difficulties and challenges, it was essential to know that these were the natural experiences of transition, difficulties that were to be expected. And in the darkest hours, I was assured by the great stories that the light would follow. Having a roadmap gave me wise guidance, hope, and faith that carried me through.

Could Homer have written the *Odyssey,* Sophocles the *Oedipus* trilogy, or Wolfram von Eschenbach the tale of *Parsifal* had they not each known the way of consciousness? Whatever the culture, language, or age, the story remains the same. I always found this comforting, and, during the darkest hours, I read and reread these great tales. There are other books I would suggest, books that inspire and reassure during difficult times. These include: Rainer Rilke's *Letters to a Young Poet,* Herman Hesse's *Siddhartha,* Alexander Daumal's *Mount Analogue,* and Viktor Frankl's *Man's Search for Meaning.* Put them in your knapsack and carry them with you. They are good nourishment when one's soul gets hungry.

2. A note of caution: impulsiveness is not helpful. We each have assumed obligations and responsibilities in our lives. It is important to conclude these with care and honor. Although there are times when one must just stop and get off, these times are rare. If impulsiveness is not helpful, neither is procrastination. What we

are seeking is a balanced and thoughtful reexamination of our lives, a careful and timely consideration of the choices at hand.

Some transitions are predictable: for example, separation and divorce, the empty nest, and a midlife transition When you see them coming, you can begin the inward turn one to two years ahead of time, contemplating the change, exploring the intention of this next part of life, reading, and, yes, planning. Other experiences, like the sudden onset of disease or loss, may thrust you directly into transition. In either instance, it is important to be careful, discerning, and wise about the movement into transition and the care of existing responsibilities.

3. We will surely encounter confusion and doubt in our transitions. It is important to identify and acknowledge these feelings as they arise. They are part of our human condition. We note their presence rather than judge ourselves, and let them go rather than attach to them. We are usually taken over by our thoughts and emotions. We identify with them so tightly that we believe we are those thoughts and feelings. Nothing could be more false and damaging than this mistaken belief. We acknowledge all thoughts and feelings that arise during transitions—pleasant and unpleasant—as part of our experience, but they are not who we are.

4. In the midst of change, it is best to find a way to live with some level of stability. Eating well, exercising, creating a comfortable living space, visiting familiar parks, following familiar routines, and maintaining and nurturing healthy friendships. These activities will be quite useful in an otherwise destabilizing time.

But there is one more critical way we can stabilize ourselves during times of change. Meditation is one of the surest ways to achieve this goal. In the natural stillness of our mind, we can experience the part of ourselves that is eternal and unchanging, strong and wise. When we make contact with this aspect of self, we feel at ease, confident, and assured. However turbulent or ephemeral our outer circumstances may seem, we can always count on its stability. Our inner self is a refuge from the storm and an assurance of the continuity of a place of peace and well-being that is always found within.

5. At times of transition, we often need assistance from others. Support can be quite helpful when wisely chosen. Choose an individual who has walked that path in his or her own life, an individual with integrity, wisdom, patience, generosity, and an open heart. It is important to know if that person has teachers of his or her own, and if that person follows a tradition whose aim is personal development and freedom. Take a close look at this individual and his or her students. Choose well. And be comfortable with shifting teachers when it seems appropriate.

Chapter 2

STAGE ONE:
The Call to a Larger Life

Nel mezzo del cammin di nostra vita
mi ritrovai per una selva oscura
che la diritta via era smarrita

• • •

Half-way upon the journey of our life,
I found myself obscured in a great forest,
Bewildered, and I knew I had lost the way

—*THE DIVINE COMEDY* – PT. 1 INFERNO – CANTO 1 – (1-3)

Dante was thirty-five years old at the midpoint of his life. But it is not the age that is important. It is that sense that we are lost in a thicket of confusion, a pathless forest. It is when we have finally lost our way, reluctantly and without intention, that we begin the journey toward truth. That is the second half of our life.

At its earliest stages, we may neither see nor feel the ground shaking nor hear our soul calling. We may have outer symptoms that herald the coming transition, yet an awareness of the great shift that is about to occur is yet unknown. We may be too inattentive to our life or too busy. The distress at hand seems resolvable on the surface. But, in actuality, the issue is far larger and deeper.

We are uneducated with regard to our inner life. That is our

13

aim here—to gain a deeper awareness and sensitivity in order to save the disaster of losing this rare and precious call to adventure, of losing the healing and wholeness that awaits us.

The Call

I've known John for decades. I first met him in the late 1970s when visiting his "wellness" center. The son of a general practice physician, he grew up in the Midwest. Following his father's path, John completed college, entered medical school, and began his medical internship. It was during that time that John first heard the disguised call to change.

It arrived on one of many seemingly uneventful days when his morning began as usual at his hospital office. He was scheduled to perform a presurgical evaluation on a patient awaiting a hernia repair. Unexpectedly, the nurse informed him that the patient would be thirty minutes late. Not accustomed to such tardiness in a hospital setting, John asked for an explanation. The nurse replied, "He is meditating, and he asked not to be interrupted until he finished."

When the patient finally arrived, John inquired about his meditation practice. Recounting a scientific paper by Harvard researcher Dr. Herbert Benson, establishing the value of meditation in the treatment of high blood pressure, Alex, a young postal employee, enthusiastically responded to his questions. John was fascinated. The only way he had learned to treat high blood pressure was with medications. Suddenly, he realized the patient was teaching the doctor about healing, and even more, the patient was teaching a way of healing that did not require the services of a physician or even medications. Instead of a morning blood pressure pill, Alex meditated.

After this brief and unexpected conversation, John began meeting with a fellow intern who introduced him to "meditation, whole foods, and other odd things." John's ideas began to change, and he discovered a new personal and professional direction. He realized that he could no longer write prescriptions for drugs that only masked the underlying problem. He chose to pursue a preventive medicine residency at the Johns Hopkins Hospital.

Subsequently, he gifted to culture the vision of *wellness* based on an out-of-print book serendipitously found on a book clearance table at the medical bookstore. Five years later, he opened the first Wellness center in Mill Valley, California. Dr. John Travis became one of the founders of the movement. His work in this field helped to fundamentally shift our way of thinking about health.

In each of our lives there are moments such as this, moments when our day-to-day life is interrupted by an unexpected event. We may lose a job or relationship, be diagnosed with a serious ailment or injury, experience the changes of aging, or, as in John's case, be unexpectedly and serendipitously introduced to a new possibility. It's like hitting the "pause" button.

If we choose to stop, listen, and explore the issue at hand, we may discover that there is more to this disruption than is apparent at first glance. The disruption may be a disguised call from our depths, a fateful call for change, a crack in our ordinary life that allows for innovation and re-creation. The timing may be inconvenient, as it usually is, but in retrospect, it proves to be precisely on time. And it is essential to pay attention, for it can easily, at great expense, be missed.

It happened in my life as well, at a seemingly most inconvenient moment. My medical career was expanding, I was writing books and speaking nationally, my family was growing, and all seemed well. One seemingly unremarkable day, I was sitting on a comfortable corner chair, reading a chapter in James Toffler's book *The Greening of America*. The chapter was titled, "The Lost Soul." As I read on, long-held tears began to burst through a carefully constructed life of busyness. That wellspring of sadness could no longer be avoided or restrained.

Sometimes tears and sadness are just momentary, the response to a particular circumstance. There are other times that they've been brewing quietly for a prolonged time, waiting to emerge from a place that is deep, wide, and chronically aching. These were those sorts of tears, that sort of sadness. It was not just a sentimental moment. It was a deep sigh of recognition, one I could no longer push away or run from. I had lost myself in the long process of creating a "secure" life as a physician. I no longer recognized who I had become.

For many months I lived in a state of darkness, groundless-ness, and confusion—what I refer to later as the "in-between" time. After slowly watching much of my life dissipate into a state of great disorder, I began speaking with a very important mentor. They say that when the student is ready the teacher appears, and certainly that was true in my case. He understood the larger intent of my situation quite quickly.

"Close your eyes and make an image of the emptiness you're feeling," he asked.

That was easy. I related to him that the image was a large hollow sphere.

He responded, "Can you find yourself in that image?"

"Yes," I answered. "I'm quite small."

"Can you let this image of yourself dissolve?" he requested.

That was easy. And then, to my total surprise, the emptiness morphed into a pervasive experience of presence and being—the dark transformed into light. I quickly shared this with him.

His response was simple, "That's who you are."

I immediately recognized his words as true for my experience. Suddenly, the confusion that had engulfed me for many months was replaced by a sense of a self that was beyond words and filled with light, ease, peace, and profound joy. It all occurred in a brief period of twenty minutes. He asked me to spend the next few weeks at a retreat center, integrating this new sense of self. I followed his instructions.

These sudden flashes of long-denied truth may not herald their full significance right away. Their timing and meaning can at first be quite unclear, as it was for me. The destiny they point toward may be veiled. We can, and many do, fall back into automatic ways of coping, denying the meaning of such moments. Yet, at these pivotal moments, something is up. It may recede for a period of time, but it is not likely to go away. A larger healing is at hand.

Consider Richard. At age forty-two he experienced his call to change in a dramatic way. His prior life followed a straight and successful path. Born into a middle-class family, he assimilated the typical American values—the importance of a good education, hard work, worldly achievement, and family and financial security. Over the years, he worked himself into a secure position as a mid- to high-level executive. He had a successful marriage, raised three children, and made a better-than-average income. Richard was a good man living a good life.

While sitting down to work on an early Monday morning, he experienced a peculiar sensation in his chest, a sensation that progressively became more worrisome. In a short time, he landed in the local emergency room. The initial evaluation strongly suggested he had suffered a heart attack, an impression that was confirmed through further testing. Lacking any obvious risk factors for heart disease or any forewarning of this serious illness, Richard and his family were shocked. They experienced a painful and jolting recognition that something had suddenly changed their lives. It was a change that would not go away.

Although the careful observation of Richard's condition during the early days of his hospital stay was unremarkable, after further testing, his physicians recommended an angioplasty, a procedure that opens up the coronary arteries to increase blood flow through the obstructed vessels. The procedure was successful, and Richard was sent home for a period of recuperation, followed by a return to work, and an effort at preventive measures, including nutrition and exercise.

I first met Richard six weeks after his heart attack when he visited my office for follow-up care. During that visit, he complained of a vague malaise that, on further inquiry, bordered on feelings of depression. Although he was looking forward to his return to work, something seemed wrong. We were to spend the next several months discussing that "something." These discussions culminated one morning when Richard, following a discussion about some of his more enjoyable childhood moments, suddenly burst into tears. He had stumbled onto one of those rare flashes of insight that can, for a few moments, provide a panoramic view of one's life. For the first time, he saw his life in a very different way. He saw that his life, however successful, had ignored many of his own needs.

He viewed himself as accomplished but unhappy, as a "strong" family man who, on closer examination, spent little or no quality time with his children, as a "good" husband who could barely recall the joyfulness that he and his wife had once shared as a couple, and as a productive worker who had forgotten how to play. As I listened to him, I recalled the prophetic opening lines of Dante's *The Divine Comedy:*

> When I had journeyed half of my life's way, I found myself within a shadowed forest, for I had lost the path that never strays. . . .

Medicine, and for that matter most of psychology, does not deal with the shadowed forest, the other side of our symptoms. Yet it is in the shadowed forest that we find the way to a larger life and a more comprehensive healing. It has always seemed peculiar to me that the medical profession, as in Richard's case, views heart disease, or any illness for that matter, as an exclusively technical problem, a kind of engineering dilemma in search of a technical solution. Most "Richards" follow the standard medical treatment and return to their former lives, relationships, and work as if nothing had happened. Depression and malaise are written off as normal "psychological" responses, and when sufficiently severe, they're treated with anesthetizing medications, permanently closing off the hard-earned opportunity to reconsider the deeper meaning of the symptoms.

According to the logic of conventional medical practice, heart disease is a biological phenomenon that is no different in one person than another, and the same formulaic treatments suffice for each case. But to ask why disease or mental distress occurs in an individual at a specific time is to point us in an entirely different direction. When we probe more deeply, the disease begins to take on a narrative, a context. It has a meaning and purpose to be discovered. It becomes a call for change.

When I first met Jennifer she was in the middle of her life, single and living with a nineteen-year-old daughter who was adopted at one year of age. The daughter, plagued throughout her life by severe learning disabilities, was unable to maintain a job, adhere to her commitments, or maintain the semblance of a responsible adult life. She had become progressively more difficult for Jennifer. For years Jennifer had ignored her own needs, focusing on maximizing her daughter's educational possibilities and supporting both of them through a variety of tenuous sales positions. Exhausted from years of personal struggle, she sought in vain for a solution, a "magic bullet" that could resolve the painful complexities of her life.

One afternoon, as she was ready to leave my office, she briefly, almost as an aside, related to me her recollection of several small pieces of a dream that had occurred the previous night. Because this dream occurred at one of the darkest and most desperate hours of her life, and because dreams can be a disguised call from the depths, I stopped and asked her to relate what she remembered. All she could recall was that in her dream, "A chicken or rooster came out of my chest." Despite additional questioning, she recalled nothing further. I next asked her about the feelings associated with this dream. She responded, "Fear! I was frightened." Next, I asked her to close her eyes and review the dream in her mind, hoping that the recollection of the feeling would help her to recall additional elements of the dream. Several seconds later, she said, "It wasn't a chicken or a rooster. It was an eagle."

This was a critical piece of information. The eagle is a symbol of spirit. I next asked her to create a visual image of the eagle and "ask it" what it had to tell her. I added to this the important instruction, "Don't demand an answer; just ask the question and be still, present, and receptive, don't have expectations." Several moments later she responded, "I can't have freedom because I'm too scared to grasp it." Jennifer then began to cry. "What's happening," I asked. She replied, "I can't look into its eyes, it's now looking at me with anger and hostility." I took her hand and asked her to imagine taking me with her as she again looked into the eagle's eyes. Her fear diminished, and she responded, "Its eyes are softening." I then suggested she ask the eagle what it needed. She responded, "It needs me to bring its head against my neck." I asked her to respond to that request. Within a few moments, she began to weep uncontrollably. "The love," she said, "it's overwhelming. Never before have I felt such love." We remained in silence for several moments, as the tears slowly stopped and a sense of peacefulness moved across her face.

I explained to her that unlike a human birth that comes through the womb or an intellectual birth that comes through the head, a spiritual birth comes through the chest, the heart space. Her dream represented the birth through her chest of a long gestating spiritual life represented by the birth of the eagle. Her acceptance and "embrace" of her spiritual aspects, her bringing the spirit in the form of the Eagle toward her body, signified the reconciliation and reunion of spirit and body. She had experienced, however briefly, an aspect of her being that could grow and flourish irrespective of her difficult life. The shift was not in the details of her life, but in how she saw and related to herself— as a victim or as the hero of a spiritual life yet to unfold.

The poet Rainer Rilke catches that moment with the following words from "Last Evening":

> Then, suddenly, the image broke apart.
> She stood, as though distracted, near the window
> and felt the violent drumbeats of her heart.

Like John's serendipitous and unexpected meeting with a patient, my own encounter with my "lost" soul, Richard's emotional and physical distress, and Jennifer's psycho-spiritual dream foretold an impending life transition. In each case, the depths were rising to the surface and announcing the arrival at a pivotal moment in life.

Each of us will experience such moments one or more times in our life—unexpected events that signal inner shifts, difficult challenges, seemingly insurmountable adversity, the simple quiet voice of despair, or a persistent sense that there is more to life. These are moments that announce that our day-to-day life is no longer in accord with our deepest intentions. They call us to great courage and urge us toward a renewed, revitalized, and larger life. They call us inward. I know it can be difficult to see those possibilities. I have been there, as will each of us. We must pay attention, lest we squander a rare opportunity to renew life.

The Soul's Thirst for Fulfillment

Where does the call for change come from? What is the source of this quiet, but insistent, voice that bursts through the surface of our well-ordered life and announces itself through mental distress, physical symptoms, or a sudden change in life's circumstances? The source is our soul, the wise source of knowing that resides at the center of our being.

As our five senses inform us about the outer world, our soul informs us about our inner world. It tells us about the state of our being. It is a barometer that measures the coherence between our authentic nature and our outer life, the gap between who we truly are and how we live our life. It speaks to us about the authentic direction and intent of our lives. It reveals our deepest and most tender yearnings and passions. It tells us when we have strayed down the wrong path and when we have taken a path true to our self.

The soul's call often reveals itself when our automatic thought patterns break down, leaving an opening, a gap, and, some may say, a vulnerability through which our innermost intentions rise to the surface. For years, we may be disturbed by physical or emotional symptoms, unaware of their true intent. The soul works like that. It lets us know that something is wrong, but it does not provide us with a precise understanding of what has gone wrong. A headache is a mere headache, depression is depression, an ulcer is an ulcer, and difficulties at the office, in a relationship, or with our children are problems to be solved or fixed, and no more than that. We have the experience but miss its greater meaning and intent.

The depth psychologist James Hillman says in *Re-Visioning Psychology*, "We owe our symptoms an immense debt . . . The right reaction to a symptom may as well be a welcoming than the laments and demands for remedies, for the symptom is the first herald of an awakening psyche which will not tolerate any more abuse. Through the symptom the psyche demands attention." If we mistake the symptom or distress as a mere surface distur-bance, we simultaneously miss the opportunity to upgrade our life. The symptom will recede, or we will accommodate to it. Life will go on as usual, as ordinary, limited by our inability to hear and respond to the soul's call.

I encountered that each day in my medical practice. Mental distress and physical symptoms are the daily fare of a physician's office. They arrive in one package. Even if the inner aspects of the symptom are unseen or unlooked for, they are always there. The immediate and exclusive goal of modern medicine, as well as to some extent psychology, is to eliminate the symptom as soon as possible rather than to linger with it, inquire, and attempt to understand its larger significance. When I listen carefully to the stories that accompanied my patient's distress, I can see and feel the energy of the two psychic forces that are simultaneously expressed.

First, I recognize the individual's urgent desire to return to life as it was, without the fear and disruptiveness of something gone wrong, a return to so-called normality. But I also recognize that another powerful force is present. We can call it an evolu-tionary impulse. At precisely the same time that we are seeking relief from outer distress, our soul, our inner life, is passionately calling us toward a life transition, toward a larger life. Both outer and inner aspects of the symptom require attention. The first effort is to relieve the immediacy of suffering. The second effort honors the call of our soul that is gently and tenderly guiding us toward a revitalized life. It is the response to that inner call that is the remedy for mental distress and suffering.

Because we cannot be certain that traditional medicine or psy-chology, in their current states of development, will address the deeper healing, we must take upon ourselves the responsibility to listen for, and respond to, the call to a larger life. After all, it is our evolutionary impulse to thrive, flourish, and fulfill our self. And it's our life that is at stake. We cannot leave that to others.

Refusing the Call

There are as many stories, and perhaps more, about those who miss the call to transition and transformation. Their lives take a different direction. Repelling from the adventure of change, they retreat back into the old and familiar. Body, mind, and spirit cease to grow, and stagnation sets in. Much as the call itself, the refusal or turning away may at first seem inconsequential, but in actuality it is life-betraying. This may show up as an acceleration of our busyness, an unconscious denial of the challenge at hand, or a prolonged period of procrastination during which a variety of ineffectual remedies are sought after. In each instance, there is a progressive erosion of the life force and an accelerated senescence.

Dennis came to speak with me about the imminent end of his ten-year marriage. It seemed important for him to tell me about it. "There was always hostility and anger. We were constantly fighting about one thing or another," he said, "I'm glad it's over. By the way," he further related, "I'm beginning to date a woman that I'm really in love with. I'm sad about the end of my marriage, but finally, with my new girlfriend, I'm really happy." We spoke briefly about the potential value of exploring the issues related to his failed marriage—his difficulties with intimacy, his excessive use of alcohol, and his explosive anger. However, he was uninterested in any further discussion of these or related issues. He found his answer, or so he thought, in another woman. I wondered what he wanted from me. Perhaps, I thought, he wanted me to affirm his new direction. But I couldn't, because to do so would be to affirm his decision to turn away from the real issues in his life—issues that could only be resolved within himself, a call from his soul that he chose to deny.

Consider another example of how individuals turn away from transition and transformation. At first glance this example may appear quite different, but it is actually very similar. Joanne visited my office after one year of fatigue, mood swings, and abdominal pain. She quickly informed me that she was using a variety of supplements and the regular services of a chiropractor and acupuncturist. On the surface she appeared to be approaching her problems with determination and thoughtfulness. However, when I began to probe more deeply into her life, searching to understand the deeper sources of her distress, I encountered an unexpected resistance.

Although she emphatically *stated* her belief in the mind-body connection, she assured me that her circumstance was exclusively a "physical problem," requiring an outside intervention of a more alternative sort. In actuality, Joanne had merely shifted from one form of treatment, conventional medicine and its professionals and resources, to another, alternative medicine, with its professionals and resources. Much as Dennis, she continued to see her distress as abnormalities to be fixed rather than understood, fixed in Dennis's case by another relationship and in Joanne's circumstance by another treatment method.

As previously discussed, *denial* and *procrastination* are two ways to refuse the call to a larger life. Dennis and Joanne demonstrate the first way, denial. They were brought to the threshold of transition by life circumstances. Their souls were calling through their usual surface language of symptoms and distress, but there was no one "home" to listen. Denial occurs when we only look at the surface appearance of things and fail to penetrate more deeply to discover their larger significance. We miss the meaning that underlies the overt appearance of distress. We ignore, avoid, or withdraw from the true issues at hand.

When in denial, we conveniently interpret a failed relationship to mean that we found the wrong person, so the answer is to find another. We interpret a failed treatment method as a need to search for an alternative. A new relationship, another treatment, a different job, a new city, different friends, vacations, acquiring new and more engaging toys, getting busy, working harder, acquiring more power and financial standing, drugs, sex, hobbies, and so on. In each instance, a Band-Aid is applied and the possibility of a larger life is lost. Denial is a psychic mechanism that enables us to completely disregard the larger reality of our circumstance. We go on as if nothing of significance has happened.

Procrastination is a second way to refuse the call. We do it by deluding our self with a series of excuses or by attempting to satisfy the call for change by "buying" time with minimal readjustments in lifestyle. We know the excuses quite well: *I can't deal with this right now, maybe next year. What about my obligations? What will they say and think? I'll get over it. This will pass.* We spend a lot of mental energy and time trying to negotiate with ourselves in order to avoid authentic living.

Attempts to carry out a few "safe" readjustments always turn out to be a compromise that fails to address the deeper issues at hand. These new arrangements are more a reconfiguration of our past than an authentic transition. It goes something like this: "If I can learn some relaxation and time-management techniques, I can probably handle this job. If I can increase my travel schedule, it will give my marriage more space and maybe we'll get along better. I'll try a self-help program, maybe that will work." Sometimes I find myself negotiating with my soul for many months, offering it a piece of what it wants if it promises to leave me alone. Attempts to make small adjustments here or there may be comforting and perhaps helpful, but they are more like rearranging furniture in the same room, when in fact what is needed is to change both the room and the furniture.

Procrastination may go on for months, and if sufficiently prolonged, it will abort the impending transition, causing us to turn away from change. Procrastination acknowledges the need for change, but tries to cheat it. Like denial, procrastination stops life by delaying or sabotaging the authentic call to a larger life. For too many years, I sat in my office listening to the stories of missed lives. "I was too busy working to play with my children." "How I wish I had the time to spend with my wife. She died last year and I miss her a great deal." "Decades have gone by, and I can't seem to remember what happened. It was like I was collecting dust. I seemed so busy, but with what?" In *Death of a Salesman,* Arthur Miller presents us with the painful image of Linda Loman, still blind to the emptiness of her life with husband, Willy, weeping at his grave the day following his suicide:

> Why did you do it? I search and search and I search and I can't understand it, Willy. I made the last payment on the house today. Today, dear. And there'll be nobody home. We're free and clear, We're free . . . We're free . . .

When we refuse the call to truth, we refuse ourselves.

To Have a Life or to Be Alive

To have a life is simple. It is given at birth. To be alive as an infant—vital, uninhibited, imaginative, and spontaneous—is natural. But to be alive as an adult is quite difficult. By then we have accumulated a personal history, ingrained beliefs, fears and anxieties, and habitual approaches to life. The words that describe an unlived life are mechanical ones like functioning, running, and working. The words that describe aliveness are full of intensity and soulfulness, words such as animated, abounding, vital, present, and passionate. Feel how each of these words affects you. The first set of words feel dead and devitalized; the second set, alive with energy.

In *Letters to a Young Poet,* the poet Rainer Rilke offers this advice to an aspiring young poet:

Go into yourself. Search for the reason that bids you to write; find out whether it is spreading out its roots in the deepest places of your heart, acknowledge to yourself whether you would have to die if it were denied you to write. This above all—ask yourself in the stillest hours of your night: *must* I write? Delve into yourself for a deep answer. And if this should be affirmative, if you meet this simple question with a strong and simple "*I must,*" then build your life according to this necessity; your life even in its most indifferent and slightest hour must be a sign of this urge and testimony to it.

Whether our soul is calling us to express ourselves through writing, teaching, healing, service in all its forms, or simply the full presence in the beauty of each moment, we must listen and carefully discover our unique, call. As the poet says, then "build your life according to this necessity." Many good ideas may arise. Each time you must ask, "Is this really what is next for me?" Yes, perhaps I would like to paint or play the piano, or try acting — all good things. But is that the essence I am seeking. Be comfortable to say, "Yes, that would be nice, but the larger movement of my life, is neither this nor that." It is deeper. Perhaps still unknown to me, but more essential. As we slowly move away from the surface and partial answers, we allow space for our deepest and most authentic call to emerge. Then our whole being will say, "I must." For this, we must first accept the call and have patience with the transitional process.

Unless we recognize and accept the call to a larger life and follow its intention, we will stop life in its tracks. We will forego transition and transformation, which is nature's way of revitalizing life. That is why this first stage of transition is so essential. Without identifying and responding to the call, in whatever unpredictable form it arrives, we cannot go further. We can only fall back into stagnation and the ailments of an unlived life.

Once we recognize the call, we must develop a deep thirst, not curiosity, a thirst. Curiosity is an intellectual interest. Thirst is an unquenchable need. If a man travels for days in the desert without water and is then offered a gold bouillon or a glass of water, he will take the water. He will take what he really needs.

It is no different with the call to a larger life. If we come to desire it with all of our being, if we develop a great thirst for truth, serenity, joy, and freedom, we are far more likely to take the appropriate remedy—the water rather than a material and meaningless substitute. So we must really want to fulfill our soul and our life. We must thirst for it.

In summary, the first and critical stage of a transformative life transition is to *recognize* and *accept* the call to change. It is to rise to the moment and grow, rather than ruminate the call from the depths, as the starting point of a new adventure and preparing to explore and learn new skills. It is to view adversity and challenge as an opportunity and teacher.

In modern times, this an act of personal heroism. Once the call to change is seen and engaged, the activities of the next five stages of transition follow in sequence.

HEART ADVICE FROM A FELLOW TRAVELER

1. Once we set off on a major life transition, there are certain aids that are of great assistance. The first is to find a mentor, if possible, who has walked this path before and can stand by you with reassurance, gentleness, and wise guidance as your transition unfolds. However, be careful. There are many who present themselves as coaches and counselors who may have "book" knowledge and even a group of clients, but lack the wisdom and presence that is necessary for an authentic mentor. Inquire carefully. Does this individual come from a lineage of teachers? Does this teacher have teachers of his or her own? Does this person "walk their talk"? Do his or her students appear serious and progressing in their efforts? Is there trust? Does this individual exude the highest integrity? Before making a decision to rely on his or her assistance, examine your prospective mentor very carefully.

2. A second important aid is the practice of meditation. This has been a traditional approach to a larger life and well-being, East and West. In actuality, this is a path rather than just a practice. It is a path of inner development that involves both formal daily meditation practice as well as an integrated approach to bringing inner stability and mindfulness into daily life. In this way, all the usual activities of daily life can become a source of learning, a source of inner development. The aim is to learn to still and focus the mind, which will allow for the breakthrough of understandings and insights that are essential components of the transitional process. I don't know how I could have successfully and authentically moved through my life transitions without the deeper wisdom that resides in the mind's natural stillness. It is of sufficient importance that throughout this book I've provided ongoing instructions to assist you in gaining this skill.

3. The problem is that our mind is continuously busy with random thoughts, feelings, and images. As a result, we cannot hear our inner voice. It can't compete with the ongoing mental monologue—the worries, judgments, recollections, fears, past regrets, and future plans. Nothing new can penetrate the mental clutter. However, if we allow our mind to settle, like silt in water, the clarity of the mind will enable us to hear our soul's call. When the inner voice is no longer obscured by the usual mental chatter, we can gain access to our authentic and knowing self. There, in the midst of the difficult moments of transition, lies the true guidance we seek and a place of rest and reassurance.

4. Weaving through most transitions is the theme of being and doing. For most of us, one component of our transition is to learn how to "be," so our everyday doing comes from a place of being rather than an incessant driving and striving. For modern individuals, learning how to be may be one of the hardest things to "do." Meditation also assists with this aspect of transition. Although, in the beginning, we will try to transfer our doing skills to meditation practice, we will soon learn that meditation is about simply being with ease in the moment. Over time, we will learn how to sustain an inner calmness that leads to a more peaceful nonreactive life as well as a reservoir of authentic wisdom. Both are key components of the transition process—learning how to be and accessing inner knowing.

5. The mythologist and teacher Joseph Campbell illustrated this with a short parable. Many of us, he said, spend decades climbing a ladder only to discover at the moment of our greatest triumph, when we finally reach the top and look over the wall, that our ladder is against the wrong wall. We realize that what we truly seek is not there. We inadvertently followed a path that would never bring us the happiness and peace we seek. Our task is to then find the "right wall" upon which to place our ladder, so that when we reach the top of the wall, we will find what we seek.

The aim of a life transition is to align our self with our authentic life purpose, and for this, we need to gain greater access to mental clarity and wisdom. That is the singular purpose of meditation—to teach us about ourselves so that we may know who we truly are and create a life from that fundamental truth. That is why meditation training is a critical part of the transitional process. Let's begin.

EXERCISE #1: CALMING THE MIND

Meditation is to the mind like the microscope is to the body. It is a tool that enables us to investigate our mind and gain a precise understanding of its structure, functioning, and capacities. This understanding enables us to take charge of our mind—calming its overactivity, allowing us to access the wisdom innate to our deeper self, and shifting the mind's operation from automatic to conscious. These three results of a progressively maturing meditation practice are essential to successfully navigating a life transition.

It is important to note that meditation as discussed here is not a relaxation technique. Yes, relaxation is one of the effects of meditation. But relaxation in itself is a transient and pleasant dulling of the mind that wears off soon after we stop using the technique. The traditional aim of meditation, and our aim here, is to establish a still, undistracted, and fully alert mind, in contrast to the dullness or dropping off of relaxation. It is that mental clarity which allows us to cultivate insight and wisdom, break through the mind's automaticity, and steer ourselves toward authenticity.

When taught and practiced correctly, meditation is neither complicated nor difficult to learn. At first, as with any other learning practice, it requires intention, effort, patience, and perseverance. However, in time it becomes as routine, simple, and automatic as brushing one's teeth each morning. We just do it out of habit, and that's a good habit. It is important to have proper instruction and guidance to assist you in shaping a practice to your lifestyle and temperament, overcoming obstacles or problems that may arise, and inspiring you at moments of discouragement.

Our purpose here is to assist you in developing a meditation practice that supports your life transition. My intent is to shape my instructions for that purpose and to keep them as simple as possible. There are six exercises. They will follow the chapters ahead and correspond to each of the stages of transition. You may linger with the first practice until you are comfortable with it, even as you read further. You can return to the next practice when you are ready. There is no hurry. Each exercise will continue to unfold for you as you work with it. So be patient and take your time with the practices. There is further detail and a practice CD included in my book on meditation training *Awake, Aware, Alive*. It can also be separately downloaded as an mp3 from [to come]. If you wish to delve more deeply into meditative practice, you can use that as a supplement.

There are two basic practices we will develop. The first is the formal daily sitting practice. The second are the practices that are integrated into daily life. The formal daily meditation practice will train you in calming the mind and cultivating stillness, which over time will enable you to develop the insights and understandings that will drive your transitional process.

The second, the daily life practice, is of equal importance. Why, because we live in the modern world. We do not live in monasteries or seminaries. So we do not have long stretches of time to practice meditation without engaging in daily life. That requires that we use all of our activities as sources of inner development. If properly approached, all of life can become part of and nourish our transitional process. Wherever we are and whatever we do becomes our practice. We will seek to bring all of life onto the path of consciousness and transition. In the exercises that follow, we will progressively build both the formal sitting practice and the daily life practices. Give them equal importance.

The Preliminaries: Time, Location, and Duration

The formal daily practice begins with identifying a time of day and place for practice. The best time is early in the morning before daily activity begins. That's when the mind is relatively quieter. Some individuals prefer to practice later in the day. That's also okay. However—a warning—most individuals begin to skip afternoon sessions when they get busy or sleepy. Choose what is best for you. It may change over time. Identify a regular location for your formal sitting practice, a space that will be free of distractions. That space will become associated with your practice and become a special space that supports the meditative and transitional process. You can choose to sit on a chair or a cushion, as is most comfortable for you. You can use a clock to glance at when you feel the session may be over, or you can use a timer if you can do so without being mentally preoccupied with the timer during the meditation practice. These are suggestions. Be flexible. The most important thing is to begin, be regular, and develop the habit of a mental "workout."

The time of the session will vary according to the practice and according to your experience. I would suggest you begin with 10 minutes. Again, be flexible. If 10 minutes is too much for you and you begin to get frustrated by your overactive mind, then try 5 minutes once or twice a day. When you think your time is complete, then glance at the clock. If there is still further time, return to the practice. If not, close your eyes for a few more minutes and then return to your daily activities. What is most important in the beginning is developing the *habit* of taking time for yourself and your inner life. As you stabilize that habit, irrespective of your session–to–session experience, you will naturally and progressively expand your session to 20 minutes.

My suggestion is that you find a comfortable sitting position on a chair or cushion. You should be sufficiently at ease so that you're not distracted by physical discomfort, but no slouching. This is an important and sacred process. Please try to sit with a straight spine, without folded legs, with your arms in your lap or on your thighs. You may practice with eyes open or closed. If open, then you can orient your vision toward a spot on the floor that follows your nose line or simply look straight ahead. We are now ready for the first set of instructions.

Recognizing Unhelpful Mental Habits

There are several unhelpful mental habits that we routinely bring into meditation. So be aware of this. The most persistent is to judge the experience as good or bad. We do not judge our meditation session or compare it to other sessions or to some imagined ideal. Meditation is about being rather than doing. So we eliminate all striving, clinging to an imagined goal or "perfect" meditation. We avoid the tendency to label our experience as a success or failure. We let go of impatience. Recognizing and eliminating these habitual psychological patterns allows our meditation to flow and serves as an act of self-compassion.

The Practice

Sit in your chosen space with your eyes closed or open. In the beginning you might find it easier to close your eyes. If you prefer your eyes open then you can either focus on a spot on the floor about four feet in front of you or look straight ahead. Relax your entire body. For the next 10 minutes, your mental focus will be on your breath. The breath is a natural experience that is always occurring in the now. By maintaining a gentle yet mindful focus on the breath, you will be training your mind in attention, concentration, mindfulness, and vigilance—all natural mental capacities. You will be learning to maintain a singular focus in the present moment without distraction. This is called one-pointedness, or merely paying attention. Over time, this simple practice will calm the mind, and that is the launching pad for the further experiences of meditation.

There are several techniques to jump-start calming the mind. Begin with 10 deep in-breaths and out-breaths. Imagine exhaling stress and tension on the out-breath and taking in calm on the in-breath. Then take a second series of 10 deep breaths, holding your breath at the end of inspiration. This hold, and don't unduly prolong it, will allow you to experience a "gap" in mental activity. That is how the mind works. When we stop our breathing, the mind naturally stops its noise. We quietly rest in this gap and experience the undistracted mind for a few moments. We remember that sense of the calm mind and carry it into the expiration and then the next inspiration followed by another hold. Repeat this 10 times before moving to the next part of the practice. This helps to both calm the coarse aspects of the noisy mind, and introduces the gap in which we briefly experience the undistracted mind. If your mind is very noisy, you can continue this aspect of the practice for the entire session. That's your choice.

Next, we allow our breathing to return to normal. Actually, we diminish the intensity of breathing as much as we can to simulate the hold on inspiration previously experienced—quiet breath, quiet mind. This may require that you take intermittent deep breaths. Don't make this a major concern; just keep the breath slow and rhythmic. Now, bring your attention to the movement of the breath in and out of your nostrils, or alternatively the rising and falling of the chest wall with the breathing cycle. The quality of attention is very important. It is more like a soft awareness of the breathing without any mental commentary. We are just aware of the breath in the moment—softly and gently. There is no judgment, no struggle, and a minimal amount of effort. The awareness rests gently on the moment-to-moment movements of the breath—noticing, observing, and letting go of the previous moment—freshness each moment.

Early on, this may require some mindfulness and effort. We use only the amount of mindfulness and effort required to maintain our focus. This may change from breath to breath or during the session. We keep our body fully relaxed and, if necessary, place some effort and discipline in maintaining awareness of the breath. Above all, relax.

The two major obstacles to this process are an overactive distracted mind or a dull mind falling into drowsiness or sleep. There are remedies for both of these obstacles that we can use until our mind is more stable. In the early phases of practice, our mind may continually wander from our focus on the breath to a thought, feeling, mental image, or physical sensation. When this occurs, we notice the distraction, and without judgment or mental commentary, we return our attention/awareness to the breath. We may have to do this over and over. That's okay. The mind will be trained over time. So do not judge the movements of your mind, just follow the instructions to return to the breath, as many times as this takes. Each time, we are practicing mindfulness. Each time is another opportunity to train the mind. Overcoming the obstacle of dullness is a bit easier. You can return to deep breathing, open your eyes, or slightly change your position. The point is to "wake" yourself up from the distraction of drowsiness and return to your focus on the breath.

Continue the practice for 10 minutes, and if possible, try to repeat it once more during the day for 5–10 minutes. It takes time to calm your mind, and if that occurs during your practice session, merely rest with wakefulness in the calmness, observing it without thought, and returning to the breath when your mind becomes overactive or dull. When the 10 minutes is complete, give yourself a few minutes to settle in and then return to your daily activities.

Integrating Practice into Daily Life

In addition to your formal sitting practice, it is important to integrate inner work into daily life by utilizing your daily experience as further opportunity to develop your mind. Begin this daily practice by stopping for a moment several times during the day, recalling your morning practice, taking a few deep breaths and holds, and settling back for a minute or two into an inner space of awareness and calm. You can do this in the midst of your usual practices. These are called "flashbacks." Briefly bring your self back to the meditative space and then return to your activities. Observe how this affects the moments to follow.

By beginning and continuing this brief practice, even if your mind is quite busy during practice, you will be on your way to developing an important aid for your life transition.

Chapter 3

STAGE TWO:
The Departure

What we call the beginning is often the end
and to make an end is to make a beginning.
The end is where we start from . . .
—T.S. ELIOT, FROM "LITTLE GIDDING"

If we are fortunate, there will come a time when the fear of change will seem less than the hopelessness of the status quo. When all our alternatives are exhausted, denial and procrastination will drop away. We'll find our self backed into a corner with only one way out. That way is to turn inward and go deeper into our self. Change is imminent. We know it. We will finally answer the call and depart on the journey.

Letting Go

When we begin the journey of transition, we're required to leave most of our baggage behind. Although this can be quite difficult, transitions must begin with endings, with necessary losses. There are three major endings that we will confront: the end of *innocence,* the end of *automatic living,* and the end of *obsolete life structures.* These will have a unique unfolding in each individual's life, but invariably, loss and new beginnings go together.

39

The End of Innocence

The end of innocence is marked by a profound turn away from a naive simplicity toward a period of uncomfortable complexity. Habitual beliefs and reactions that long determined the course of our life no longer work. Our life experience shifts from a monotone to a complex symphony.

Like Adam, we're tossed out of the proverbial Garden and into the intricacies of life, with all of its contradictions, its light and its dark. Childhood love, which was as simple and innocent as "Roses are red, violets are blue," is replaced by the puzzling and perplexing issues of adult intimacy. Career choices that once seemed certain are now open to question. Values and lifestyles taken from family and culture are reconsidered. Nothing seems to be as it was. We can no longer rely on simple answers. They don't work. There is no solid ground to stand on. Life is now more complex, intense, and uncertain. Adrienne Rich expressed this breakdown of primal innocence in her poem "November 1968":

> You're what the autumn knew would happen
> after the last collapse
> of primary color
> once the last absolutes were torn to pieces
> you could begin

You could begin, as the poet Pablo Neruda said, to write the first line, the first line of *your* life. It is the point of embarkation where what you have become under the influence of others gives way to the polychromatic essence of who you are.

The End of Automatic Living

Once we've passed through the gateway of transition, we begin to question everything. Our lives, which once seemed freely chosen, are now seen for what they actually are: the result of tenacious childhood programs unknowingly inherited from others. We always thought we were free to do whatever we wanted. Now, to our astonishment, we discover that our ideas and actions contained very little that was new. Whether we followed the dictums of parents, early teachers, or culture, or rebelled against them, we were still trapped in a conditioned set of behaviors that lacked consciousness and choice. Authentic freedom, we now discover, was something we never had. With this realization comes the beginning of the end of automated living.

There is a deflating disillusionment that comes with the discovery that much of what we designed our lives around, believed in, fought for, insisted on, and would almost die for now seems nothing but a silly mistake. At first, there is the recognition of how narrow and imprisoned our lives have been, how we deluded ourselves into mistaking the compelling imperatives of our youth for free will. We begin to insist that these fixed formulas and rigid childhood patterns no longer govern our thoughts and actions.

But it is not simply a question of wishing. These automated patterns are tenaciously embedded in our psyche. When we think we are finally free of them, they reassert themselves once again, hiding in a new set of "clothes." We think something new is emerging, but it is only our old patterns in disguise. Once again we recognize these constricting patterns, and once again we rededicate our self to letting go and becoming liberated from their influences.

How confused and lost we may feel, as we let go of what previously defined our life. All is changing. Life first becomes more clouded and muddled. Where there were once answers, there are now only questions. Where we could easily reach into our minds and quickly count on what seemed to be a clear and decisive response, we now feel somewhat immobilized, uncertain, and hesitant to act. What are we to do? What can we be certain of?

Is there any steady ground that we can stand on? The more we learn, the more we discover how little we really know. Life, which once seemed simple and clear, now appears more as a mysterious and almost impassable labyrinth.

The end of automatic living and the emptying out of all that is not our authentic self can be a difficult and confusing loss that takes time and requires fortitude. We have to be willing to live with difficult emotions, questions without answers or solid ground, and even with some anxiety. This requires patience, self-compassion, and knowledge of the stages of transition.

The End of Obsolete Life Structures

The progressive ending of naive innocence and automatic living is the basis for the third ending, the voluntary dismantling of *obsolete life structures.* Letting go of the pillars of our previous existence is the most painful of the three endings. As children, we had no options. We borrowed our beliefs and values from our families and culture. As young adults, we built lives based on these ideas. We committed ourselves to careers, marriages, and families with little or no understanding of who we were, what we were doing, and why we were doing it. Everyone applauded, and our families and culture had its way. Regardless, there still remains a youthful soul, silenced by the needs and perspectives of others, imprisoned in the structures of a world that was more imposed than personally chosen, yet still yearning to fulfill its destiny.

We invariably discover the need to deconstruct what was never our own. The field must be laid barren so that it can be available for the new growth. Our false self must leave its temporary home. Dismantling the past, whether it's piece by piece or all at once, is never easy. The past served a purpose. It helped us survive childhood, minimize the adversities of youth, please others, and fit in. The past was secure and familiar and more comfortable than the risks of the unknown. Regardless of its inadequacies, it worked to keep us alive and secure. As a result, the past has a strong hold on us. Remember the moment in the quiz show when the contestant had to decide whether to stop with the money already won, or risk it all in order to find out what was behind the next door? The moment between the comfort of what is and the risks of what might be is the same tension that makes the process of dismantling outdated lifestyles so difficult. We know what we need to do, but should we risk it all for the unknown?

It must be emphasized here that the process of letting go may be a progressive one that takes place over months or years. As previously mentioned, we have responsibilities and obligations to others that, at times, must be honored until they are complete. At other times, the choice is different, and a complete break is possible. Whether gradual or rapid, you must act with discernment, sensitivity, and a compassionate heart. That does not mean that everyone will like your choices. They may not. However, it is likely that with the passage of time, they will understand and appreciate what you've accomplished.

Dismantling one's outdated life may require letting go of important life structures—marriages, careers, and lifestyles—structures we may be deeply attached to. There may be experiences and people that can no longer be part of our lives. I recall Henry David Thoreau's words upon his departure from his beloved Walden Pond in *Walden:* "I left the woods for as good a reason as I went there. Perhaps it seemed to me that I had several more lives to live, and could not spare any more time for that one." That is how it is. Everything has its time, and it is important to know when something is over and to let go in a timely manner.

The ending of innocence, automatic living, and the dismantling of obsolete life structures are marked by loss, confusion, and disillusionment. These discomforts are the price we must pay if we wish to depart on the journey to a larger life. What we leave behind will, over time, fade in its importance as a new, larger, and more satisfying life replaces what was lost. The old slowly shifts to the background, loses value, and significance as one's new and more authentic identity emerges in the foreground, taking on its own value and importance.

Endings, Losses, and Grieving

Over the years, I've discovered that I have less of a tendency to attach to particular events and experiences. I've become more accepting and appreciative of the ebb and flow of life. Life seems more fluid, more open to change and new possibilities. But it has not always been this way. I, like you, have known attachments, endings, losses, and grief, and still do.

It's difficult to let go of holding on. We can be quite passionate and attached to people, our homes, our valued possessions, and our way of life. It seems to me that much as there is a part of our soul that yearns for adventure and change, there is another part that seeks permanence, a constancy of people and things, and wants to hold on to what is, regardless of its appropriateness or the reality of the universal principle of impermanence.

T. S. Eliot once said, "Humankind cannot bear very much reality." The reality he was speaking of is the impermanence of all things. Yet this is a truth of life that we increasingly arrive at through living. It is driven home most emphatically when we pass through the endings that characterize the departure stage of transition. I have learned to respect and honor this part of my being. I now know that whenever I must give up the familiar, my heart laments the loss. I cannot bypass that process. I must acknowledge, accept, and move on from the sadness and poignancy that is part of awakening to a larger and more authentic life.

Working in a healthy way with sadness and loss means to nei-ther ruminate on these emotions, nor repress or suppress them. It is more like acknowledging a friend passing on the street and moving on. Our emotions are part of our human condition. They arise, abide, and fall. But they are not who we are. They are as impermanent as all else. So we learn to greet them without judg-ment or reaction and let them go on their own, as they will. In this way, we fully experience the present in the moment without holding on, elaborating, pushing away, or in any other way react-ing to the presence of challenging emotions. Much as the ocean allows waves to form and disperse under their own power, so can we allow our mental movements to come and go on their own without disturbing the depths of our being.

I suspect that we will never arrive at a time in life when loss does not feel like loss, or the letting go of an outdated life does not leave us with sadness. Yet, simultaneously, there is a natural antidote arising in heart and mind that progressively softens attachment and eases loss. There is an inner well-being that pro-gressively reveals itself as we settle into our inner life, discovering there a natural joy and peace. This is the gift of the meditative approach to a life transition.

The second stage of transition, the departure, is a wonderfully difficult time. The difficulty is sustaining loss. The wonder is what it teaches us.

Heart Advice from a Fellow Traveler

1. Stepping through the gateway of transition is an irreversible act. Once you've passed through, you will already know too much. You can't turn back. So when this course is chosen, it will natu-rally unfold. One's energy shifts from attachments to the past to an uneasy, yet exciting, adventure into the unknown. The diffi-culty of saying good-bye and grieving loss will progressively come to an end, and the journey toward a revitalized life lies ahead. Your thoughts will increasingly be with the passage awaiting you rather than with what's been left behind. As the bible says, "Let the dead bury the dead."

2. At this early stage of transition, it is important to know that the sadness and loss of necessary endings already contain the seed of your unknown future. It's as if your soul has already and always known, in its deepest places, the life that awaits you, as you begin your tentative steps toward this unknown. Have trust and faith, as those before you have had, that your dark and confused moments contain the hidden essence of the life to come. It is encoded in your being. Be patient and allow it to naturally reveal itself.

3. Transitions call upon all of our energy. Although we may be preoccupied with the many uncertainties that surround us, it is essential to take care of our health so that, at the other end of our transition, we can enjoy our new life with a healthy mind and body. My prescription is simple: daily exercise, wholesome nutrition, joyful surroundings, and regular meditation and/or yoga. A program such as this will keep your mind and body strong. Don't negotiate with yourself; simply create a set routine and do it each day, whether you like it or not. This is not a luxury. It's about surviving and prospering through the many stresses of a transition. Take it as you would a physician's prescription.

4. The inner journey is best taken with the support of a wise teacher. However, even with the guidance of a teacher and good wishes of friends and family, no one can do it for us. Growth and development occur through self-discovery and self-education. We must be able to listen to our self and our life. For this, we require more solitude than we usually allow in day-to-day-life.

Transition is a special time. So cut back a bit on your busyness and allow time for reflection and contemplation.

5. As we learn how to better navigate our lives, change will become more proactive. Proactive change, or what is perhaps more aptly called intentional change, is reserved for the individual who, through desire and effort, has gained the resources, capacities, and insights that allow for a thoughtful and deliberate movement though life. It is one thing to "fall" into or answer the distressful call to a transitional process, which is usually what happens with our first transition; it is something else entirely to anticipate and plan it. The difference is in willing one's life rather than reacting to it. We are learning. We are learning the skills of intentional and conscious living.

EXERCISE #2: THE HANDSHAKE MEDITATION

In the previous chapter you began the very important effort to calm your overactive mind. The focused breathing practice is a foundational practice. It calms coarse mental activity, trains attention, concentration, mindfulness, and vigilance, and it is the entranceway to the natural stillness and clarity of mind. This foundational practice may continue for many months or longer. Regardless of our progress in calming the mind, insights and wisdom may break through at any time, greatly assisting us in navigating a life transition.

The two major obstacles to calming the mind are the overactive mind and the dull mind. In this practice session, we focus on the obstacle of an overactive mind. In Exercise #1, we used several breathing techniques—deep breathing coupled with breath-holding and mindful breathing. These rely on the unique relationship between breath and consciousness, enabling us to progressively still mental activity. These methods relate to random mental activity as unwanted intruders. However, in order to progress, it is important to gain a subtler understanding of mental activity and a corresponding capacity that allows the mind to naturally maintain stillness. This approach, the handshake meditation, recognizes that mental movements are a natural part of the mind and become distractions not because of their presence, but because of how we *relate* to them.

In Exercise #1 we learned important tools for cutting off the intrusion of random mental activity. In this exercise, we are going to work with intrusive mental activity with a "handshake." In other words, we are going to cease seeing mental activity as intrusive, as if it were an enemy to be conquered. Instead, we are going to accept mental activity—thoughts, feelings, mental images, and sensory experiences—as natural expressions of our human condition.

So how do we relate to mental activity in a way that both acknowledges and accepts its presence as part of our human condition and, simultaneously, without repressing or suppressing mental activity, maintain mental calm? How do we fully experience our mental activity without being taken over by it? That is the subtlety we must understand to arrive at an effortless and natural still mind.

THE LIFE CYCLE OF RANDOM MENTAL ACTIVITY

To understand how to achieve these goals, we must understand how the mind works. Throughout life we build a storehouse of memories. That storehouse is in our unconscious mind. Memory's entire content would be too much for any mind to deal with all at once. However, when stimulated by a current event small pieces of related memory rise to the surface of consciousness. They are then experienced as thoughts, feelings, or mental images. Like waves rising and falling in the sea, the natural life span of a single blip of mental activity is less than 200 milliseconds. If we do not "react" to them, the rapid appearance and disappearance of mental activity would elude our attention.

But that is not how it is. As soon as a thought enters consciousness, we automatically react to it, altering its brief and innocuous life span. We do this in a number of ways. First, we objectify and solidify this movement. Thoughts are mere neuroelectrical "blips." They have no actual solidity. Left alone they arise, lose their energy, and rapidly dissipate. However, we immediately react to their appearance—attaching, holding, and freezing them in place. It's as if the ocean could catch and hold a wave at its peak and sustain its form. The ocean cannot do that, but a mind that is accustomed to stopping, holding, and sustaining transient mental activity can do this. And it seems quite natural. However, what we are doing is artificially distorting the natural flow of the mind. We are solidifying and extending what otherwise is an intangible and brief mental experience.

But there is more. Once we freeze a fragment of memory, we further elaborate it into a mental story. Then, we label the thought or feeling as desirable or undesirable, attaching to it or pushing it away—both of which further freeze it in place. We then add a context to this thought, turning it into an imagined story constructed of fragments of past experience that are available for rumination. That is how a brief neuroelectrical blip is turned into an intrusive and distracting mental event.

The truth is that it is like a night dream. Nothing is really happening. We make it all up. As we come to understand and learn how to deal with this tendency of the mind, the mind calms down on its own, naturally and without effort. The energy and influence of these mental blips dissipate and disappear as we stop reacting and personalizing every movement of our mind. And how do we do this? We simply observe and understand, over and over, what is happening, and with consciousness, intent, and discipline, we reverse the process that creates endless, useless, and anxiety-producing mind talk.

The Practice

So let's begin. I suggest that you extend your sessions to 15–20 minutes to continue your existing foundational practice and allow time to add this new approach. Begin with Exercise #1 as described in the previous chapter. This is your ongoing way to calm the coarse overactivity of your mind. After 5–10 minutes of your basic practice, I suggest that you begin to relate to the talkative mind in this more subtle way. Previously, we abruptly cut off mental activity that intruded on our mindful attention to the breath. Now we will handle these distractions somewhat differently.

We will view them as normal activity of the mind, a part of the way human consciousness works. We will greet this mental activity as we would greet a very casual friend, say hello, shake hands, and move on. The key is to cease reacting to them. The minute we notice the appearance of a thought, feeling, or mental image, *we acknowledge it, say hello, and then leave it to go on its way alone.* We do not judge it—like it or dislike it. We do not elaborate it with a further story. We do not extend it. We do not embrace it or suppress it. Like the passivity of a mirror toward the random appearances on its surface, we take no interest, leave them alone, and let them go on their natural way. As they dissipate we resettle our self in mindful breathing.

We make no big deal about what passes through our mind, anymore than an ocean cares about the waves on its surface. The arising and falling of thoughts is natural; It is not a source of interest or concern to us. It is insubstantial and more dream-like than real. It takes time to retrain the mind to reassume its natural ways. Our conditioned mind invariably tries to capture and "work" with what arises. That's okay. When you notice this, practice with that situation by changing your attitude from reactivity to neutrality. If it is very difficult to work in this manner, then return to the original breathing exercises, simply cutting off mental activity once it arises.

It is important to note here that our cultural training has placed great weight on every feeling and thought that arises in consciousness. There may be a time to psychologically analyze the source of certain troubling and persistent thoughts or feelings, That is okay and perhaps helpful at times. But there is also a time to stop indulging in the exploration of early wounds and work with the root of the problem, the manner in which our mind has learned to identify our self with our thoughts, feelings, and past history, setting off an endless chain of rumination and self-negativity.

Using this more subtle approach, rather than struggle with intrusive mental activity, we acknowledge, greet, and let go. We allow it to dissipate on its own. We learn to dis-identify and de-energize what are, in actuality, simple and unelaborated mental movements. We are reversing the process of elaborating and adding our history to mere mental blips. When we gain experience in seeing the mind and its movements as they actually are and letting them be, we will be more able to work with the difficult thoughts and emotions of transition while discovering a place of peace and refuge that underlies these mere movements.

You can move back and forth between these two meditative approaches: mindful breathing and the "forced" return from mental distractions and the more gentle and natural meditation in which we emphasize neither reacting to, judging, nor developing a "relationship" with these mental distractions. The important point is to use the approach *that works for you* and alternating your approaches as suited to your moment-to-moment practice. Not only are we trying to calm the mind through these methods and approaches, but we are also gaining insight into how the mind works. We are learning how we take a simple mental blip and turn it into a distracting and disturbing mental event. When you are finished with your 15–20 minute meditation, slowly return to your daily activities.

Integrating Practice into Daily Life

I would like to add another activity to your daily life practices. We are going to practice and strengthen mindfulness through the opportunities that arise throughout the day. We will accomplish this by transforming selected activities into "mini-meditations." Here and there during the day stop for a moment and bring your full attention to a singular activity at hand. This could be eating a meal, tying shoelaces, walking, working on your computer, or any other experience. Much like the practice of mindful breathing, we use the chosen activity as our focal point, maintain our focus, and when our mind wanders, bring it back to the focal point.

You can do this for several minutes several times a day. Without disrupting your daily activities, you are strengthening your "mental muscles" of attention, concentration, vigilance, and mindfulness. Some individuals do this randomly throughout the day while others will choose an activity ahead of time, like eating lunch. This daily "practice" activity will multiply your efforts to train the unruly mind.

Learning to calm the mind will enable you to deal with intrusive and difficult thoughts and feelings that arise during the stages of your life transition, as well as other challenges or adversities. Can you imagine what it would be like when you develop confidence in letting go instead of reacting to what appears in your mind? Can you imagine what it would be like when the development of this inner confidence results in your no longer fearing your self—your thoughts, feelings, and mental images? Can you imagine the ease that will begin to pervade your mind with the loss of fear and anxiety, which are the results of a mistaken reaction to mental appearances? As this new skill develops, you simultaneously become more capable of dealing with all intrusive mental activity, particularly the feelings of loss and grief that arise as you let go and depart on your transition, and you will be better prepared to work with the varied emotions that arise in the next stage: the in-between time.

Chapter 4

STAGE THREE:
The In-Between Time

Where do we come from? Where are we going?
What is the meaning of life? That is what every heart is
shouting, what every head is asking as it beats on chaos.
—NIKOS KAZANTZAKIS, *SAVIORS OF GOD*

Once we let go of the outdated structures of our life and depart on the life-changing journey of transition and change, we find ourselves entering the *in-between time.* That special time of transformation and renewal has been described in many ways throughout the ages.

It is the time that Buddha sat under the Bodhi tree discovering the true nature of life, the days that Jesus spent in the desert confronting his demons and communing with the divine, the solitude of the Native American vision quest, the revelatory excursions of the Shaman, and the simple wandering of the Hindu Sanayasin.

For you and me, it is the moment when ordinary time is suspended, as we move forward on our noble journey of self-discovery. It's a special and sacred time during which the essential elements of our lives will slowly and naturally reshape themselves. It is a time of revitalization and renewal. It holds the promise of a second birth into a deeper and more fulfilling life.

Incubation

The in-between time is our time of incubation. It's the interval between the life we once lived and the one to follow. It's a period of fluidity, exploration, and reflection. Stripped of the intransigence of previous identities, emptied of expectations, and less subject to the conventions of social life, we begin to float free in the uncharted territory of our inner life.

On the surface it may seem that we are inactive and unproductive. Society and our friends may look upon us with a compassionate, yet misguided, concern for our mental health. But this is not a period of inactivity. It is a time when the center of activity has shifted from outside where it is most apparent, to inside where it is far less so. This retreat from our usual worldly activities signifies the onset of a period of intense personal reflection. It is our personal vision quest. It is the time we are given to reengage the timeless human process of self-renewal.

We are not accustomed to this mode of existence. One day we're living a normal life, and the next day we're no longer sure who we are. We discover the fragile and transient foundation upon which our seemingly well-constructed life and identity was built. Change can be sudden and dramatic, or it can progress at a more measured pace. In either case, the ground upon which our life was built begins to shift and move. We search for solid ground upon which to place a foothold, and fail to find it. We discover that we are unsure, uncertain, and yet, we are simultaneously pregnant with new possibilities, possibilities that can only emerge from this emptiness, this seemingly empty, but actually very alive, void. It is there that our new life is incubated.

Confusion and Groundlessness

It can come as quite a shock that much or all that we once called our life may now seem strangely unfamiliar and out of place. Who was that person? How could I have lived that way? How could everything fall away so easily and quickly? The loss of our sense of identity is difficult. It strips us to the core. We lose the identities through which we conducted daily life as well as the security and familiarity of comforting routines.

What is left is a difficult and poignant sense of emptiness and disorientation. We find ourselves floating free with no rudder and no prevailing winds. We might feel as if we are entering a personal abyss. But the truth is that we are actually leaving one. We feel like we are courting insanity. But the truth is that we are becoming sane. Faith is important here. So please stay with me to the end of our journey.

We may experience the in-between time with varying levels of intensity that may seem to change day to day. When experienced to its fullest, the in-between time is a time of groundlessness. We've dissolved the old forms and sacrificed a false self in order to discover an authentic self.

Habituated to seeking and finding answers, we are now stymied. Accustomed to objectives, goals, and clear directions, we are frustrated and confused. Misunderstood by others, we begin to question our journey. Nothing seems to make sense. We can't go back. We can't go forward.

For decades our lives have collected dust. Now we live a decade every ten minutes. In the past, we lived anywhere but in the present moment. Now that is all we have. We are forced to live in the here and now, and that is a gift and blessing, however difficult it may seem. From the perspective of conventional values, we have been overtaken by a certain kind of madness.

We are tested as never before. Fear, confusion, doubt, aloneness, and moments of despair are the inner dragons we will meet. It's like leaving a familiar shore by rowboat and landing in the middle of a body of water without a shoreline in sight. The great writer Tolstoy described it this way: "I felt that something had broken in me upon which my life had always rested, that I had nothing left to hold onto . . ." It is the dark night of the soul. In T. S. Eliot's words:

> In order to arrive at what you do not know
>   You must go by a way that is the way of ignorance.
> In order to possess what you do not possess
>   You must go by the way of dispossession.
> In order to arrive at what you are not
>   You must go through the way in which you are not.

It is precisely these difficult feelings, this letting go, that assists us in discovering the truth of our lives. We realize that knowingly and unknowingly we overvalued and came under the influence of the opinions and views of others and the outside world, while undervaluing our own inner knowledge and passion. Where we thought we were being ourselves, we find we were living a borrowed life that never quite fit.

Without looking into and through these painful feelings, we cannot understand the truth of our life and turn toward who and what we are. Our insight is obscured and limited by the transient pleasantries of life, amusements, distractions and numbing entertainment, avoidance of our darker places, and the refusal to listen to our inner call. But that is no longer possible.

The poet John Keats said, "Do you not see how necessary a World of Pains and troubles is to school an Intelligence and make it a Soul?" Emptiness, loss, and chaos is a lens we have never looked through. It is a perspective that allows for deep looking and deep listening. It is a view cleaned of the obscuring layers of habitual patterns and false identities. We can finally see what is, as is. We can finally discover, piece by piece, who and what we are.

Aha!

In these moments of emptiness/fullness important insights spontaneously arise. We learn about the impermanence of things—money, status, careers, roles, and power. We learn about humility, trust, authenticity, living in the moment, and holding our center. Then suddenly, often quite unexpectedly, we catch a glimpse of a far more fundamental self that lacks labels, distinctions, concepts, or boundaries. A self that the Yogis call the *Atman,* the Buddhists call the *Original Face,* the Christians call *Christhood,* and the Alchemists call the *Gold.* Once experienced, the distinction between what one does and who one is begins to collapse into a seamless harmony.

There is a slow and cautious acceptance that something new is at hand. The dark confusion is punctuated by moments of light, a deepening sense of self-confidence and self-reliance. We can begin to see how the illusionary dependence on relationships, career, fame, and power as the sources of security and happiness. We become increasingly convinced that what we're discovering within what we have always and unsuccessfully searched for on the outside.

It is in this parenthesis in our lives, the in-between time, when the past is wiped clean, that we begin to sense from our heart our own melody, our own voice. What is my unique nature? What is my deepest truth? What are the gifts I bring to life? What am I passionate about? What conveys joy and love, meaning, and purpose? On what foundation shall I build a new life?

Joseph Campbell instructed us to "Just follow your bliss." Of course, he was not referring to temporary pleasures, but rather to the deep enduring joy that resides in the center of our being. To do so, we must first meet, in the words of the poet Derek Walcott in "Love After Love," "The stranger who has loved you all your life, whom you ignored for another, who knows you by heart." In the midst of the in-between time, we are certain, at the most unexpected moments, to meet the forgotten stranger—our essential self. And that is where we begin, once again, to write the story of *our* life.

As the in-between time draws to an end, we slowly and tentatively begin to assert our newly discovered unique nature, separating and distinguishing our self from acquired modes of being that are both alien to our nature and self-betraying. We think for ourselves, find our own ways, and bear allegiance to values that are self-chosen. And we may be required to say "no" again and again to those who would distract us from our journey. We do so because in the poet David Whyte's words in "Enough" we find ourselves finally "opening a life, we have refused, again and again, until now, until now." We can refuse it no more. Our consciousness awakens from its deep slumber. Life begins to vibrate with new energy. The period of incubation, the precious in-between time, its purpose fulfilled, slowly comes to an end.

Heart Advice from a Fellow Traveler

1. Here are some thoughts that may help soften the in-between time.

Every feeling you encounter—sadness, frustration, confusion, anger, despair, depression, and others—is *appropriate and legitimate*. These feelings do not indicate that something is wrong. They indicate that you are moving through the dark night of the transition and preparing for the light ahead. These feelings should not be avoided, repressed, suppressed, or acted out. They can be worked with in day-to-day life, as is done with the handshake meditation.

Passing thoughts and feelings, however difficult, must be a respected part of your humanity. Learn to greet them with a non-judgmental hello, let them be, and then let them go on their own.

They are not who you are. They are merely visitors from memory passing through consciousness for a few moments. They are mere neuroelectrical discharges stored in brain memory.

When left alone, these "brain bleeps," manifesting as thoughts and feelings, dissipate in less time than the space between two beats of the heart. It takes practice to learn to acknowledge yet dis-identify with movements of memory. But as you master this skill, you cease fearing your thoughts and feelings. They do not affect you any more than surface waves affect the ocean depths. Progressively, you cease fearing your self, and that is quite an accomplishment.

2. Transition and transformation cannot be fully accomplished without reflection, contemplation, and meditative practices. That invariably requires greater solitude. There are many ways to create solitude, even in a busy life—short moments of meditation during the day, a morning or day each week unhooked from technology, or a quiet meal alone.

3. Be patient with this precious in-between time, and do not act until your heart and head have reached a sustained feeling of clarity. Clarity of this sort has a steadiness and confidence about it. It is quite different from a fleeting taste of clarity. It takes time to evolve. A premature effort to conclude this stage will abort the natural unfolding of your transition. You will know when you are about to enter the next stage of transition. You will know by the certainty, calmness, and persistence of your new vision.

4. You need to survive this period of time to be able to take full joy in your new life. So begin a regular exercise program, eat well, and gravitate toward supportive friends and peaceful environments.

5. It is not necessary to take your entire life apart. It is best to adjust your transition to the essential realities of your life. We often have responsibilities toward others, and we must be carefully to consider these circumstances. Although the busyness related to work could hinder your ability to find quiet time, so can an acute lack of funds. Holding on to some of your old life structure may preclude entering the in-between time stripped bare, but in modern times, that may be the most appropriate approach. With skill and thoughtfulness, consider your situation carefully, and then decide what is best for you.

6. It is important to reflect on the central theme of your transition. When I passed my fiftieth year I concluded, after much meditation and reflection, that the central theme of my transition was the shift from doing to being. My family completed and my career established, I needed to learn to simply be in the moment and enjoy the richness of life as it is happens. What will be the central theme of your transition? Be patient; the answer does not arrive in one day.

7. The in-between time is the pivotal stage of transition. It cannot be rushed. There will be back and forths, moments of breakdown and breakthrough, and even moments of boredom. It is important to note that the stages of transition are not distinct. They often overlap. As you progress through the in-between time, it will be helpful to recall the inspiration of your call to change.

8. Transitions don't go on forever. If your transition gets stalled, if the in-between time goes beyond six to nine months or your feelings are so intense that they immobilize you, get help. Help should be in the form of a skilled counselor. Choose one who is old enough to have moved through at least one major transition, is sufficiently broad-minded to see your feelings as a call from your soul rather than an illness, and is willing to join you in your transition rather than imposing upon you his or her vision of what it ought to be. Make sure your uniqueness is being honored and your mind, body, and spirit are treated as a single unit. There are other ways to get help. These include workshops, retreats, related webcasts, and books.

9. I've found keeping a journal to be quite helpful, particularly during periods of intense reflection. Journaling is like speaking with a close friend. It helps you more clearly see and understand both the process and content of your experience. There is no better time to begin a journal than during a transition.

10. When we descend into the darkest hour, we are approaching the final moments of the in-between time. Paradoxically, when all seems lost and there is nothing further to lose, all is found. Extraordinary flashes of insight can suddenly transform the darkest hours into moments of great clarity, and perhaps even ecstasy. And when the dark begins to lift, there is a slow release of tension, an acute sense of aliveness, a newfound feeling of confidence and competence, and an eagerness to move forward. The period of incubation is over, and your new life is ready to unfold. It is time to breathe more freely, to rest, to look more assuredly toward the future, and to envision the specifics of your return to the day-to day world. You will not return the same as you left. You will leave the in-between time wiser and more fully yourself, taking with you the lessons learned that will soften the way through future transitions.

EXERCISE #3: RESTING IN STILLNESS

The in-between time calls upon all of your resources. This first encounter with groundlessness can be quite difficult. It is of great assistance to recognize and stabilize a ground within that will serve as an anchor during this stage of transition and as a source of inner stability and well-being throughout your life. Exercises #1 and #2 are the foundation for cultivating an inner ground of silence and stillness.

The first two exercises are called "meditation with support." They rely on a support (in this case, the breath) to calm and stabilize the mind. Meditating with support is an important foundation for further practice. However, continuing to exclusively rely on this method, stops the natural progression of your meditation. There is a judgment, based on your particular practice experience, as to when you practice meditation with support and when you move toward meditation without support. You may go back and forth between these two approaches in a single session. Over time, as your mind stabilizes, you will gravitate toward meditation without support.

What's meditation without support? It is a practice that no longer relies on a focal point. It is a shift from focused concentration, bringing attention and concentration to a focal point, toward a natural resting in an open, spacious, undistracted, clear awareness. That awareness is the basic ground of our mind, the natural resting place of the mind. The aim is to rest with ease and naturalness in the self that underlies our mental commentary.

Although the best understanding will be attained through experience, it is of value to further describe the awareness I am discussing. Think of it as the surface of a mirror. Just as the mirror's surface allows images to come and go without reaching out or reacting to them, our natural state of awareness experiences all of the appearances in the mind—thoughts, feelings, images, objects, sensory experiences, and so on—passively and nonjudgmentally. This awareness is alert, but it not reactive. It observes and notices, but adds nothing. That is how our mind naturally works moment to moment, experience to experience. Consciousness is a continuum of experiences—mental activity—that appear and dissipate within the ground of a stable, unchanging, simple awareness.

This simple awareness is an effortless presence, unlike the practices that use a focal point for support. It is an easeful and natural state of being, nothing more and nothing less. Because it is so simple and natural, it may be difficult at first to recognize and then to stabilize this natural state. We are so accustomed to attaching to and getting lost in the content of the mind. We cannot see what is always there. The noisy mind obscures this natural self much like clouds obscure the sun.

Look at it another way. Usually our ego, our sense of I, is the "experiencer" of our life. It is constantly enmeshed with all that it experiences, adding old stories and reacting with habitual patterns of behavior. However, our basic state of being is an underlying, disinvested awareness. It's a simple passive observer that, as an alternative to the complex ego, experiences and witnesses a continuously moving world just as it is, without shaping or distorting it through the influence of memory. This does not mean that we cease responding to the experiences of daily life, but rather that we relate and respond to them in a manner that is both accurate and appropriate.

Not only does this practice help to still the mind, it also trains our mind in another very essential way. It trains us to use the handshake meditation as a way to reverse our tendency to enmesh ourselves with the usual barrage of mental activity. We learn how to experience life fully, its pleasures and challenges, without reactivity or attachment. We can be present and completely experience all of life, but do so from a place of peace, calm, nonreactivity, and nonjudgment. Not every meditation or moment in life will be quiet and calm, but what's possible is the cultivation of a remarkable and growing steadiness amidst the experiences of day-to-day life. That ability is much more significant than the amount of noise or calm experienced in one meditation session or another. This growing capacity serves as an anchor of stability in transitional times.

There is little more to say at this point. It is better to begin to explore it in practice. I suggest you continue with your 20-minute sessions, incorporating the handshake approach to distracting thoughts. If this is insufficient to still coarse mental activity, then just pull your mind back to the breath and hold it there with mindfulness. When you attain some level of mental calm, you can most easily progress to meditation without support. This could take months, occur quite rapidly, or come and go session to session or within a single session. There is no hurry. Be patient.

There are some individuals who actually find it easier to do the open awareness meditation without support. If that is you, you can use this as your preferred or starting practice. More likely it is not. So, if this is not you, then you should continue to rely on the breathing practices until there is a natural shift to meditation without support.

The Practice

Begin this practice by resting in a natural ease and calm. In your usual practice position, relax and rest in a basic presence and beingness. Just be natural. Simply allow yourself to experience whatever is happening as it happens without doing anything at all. Make that your intention. That may seem easy, but it isn't. Almost immediately, you will notice how your mind tries to manipulate and become enmeshed in every mental experience. The mind adds stories—likes, dislikes, context taken from the past, and so on. The mind can't leave things as they are.

That is a very strong mental habit. In this open meditation without support, your intention is to give up control, to surrender to the way things actually are. Thoughts, feelings, and sensory experiences are what they are, no more and no less. Nothing is added, and nothing is taken away. If you are able to allow the mind to move without grasping onto each movement, it will effortlessly develop, on its own, a natural calm. You will also reinforce the central aim of the handshake practice—to reverse the habit of reacting to every mental experience in meditation and in daily life.

Simply allow yourself to experience whatever is happening as it happens without doing anything at all. This may seem easy. It isn't. You will note almost immediately how your mind tries to manipulate and become enmeshed in every mental experience. That is a very strong mental habit. In this open meditation without support, your intention is to give up control, to surrender to the way things are. If you are able to increasingly allow the mind to move without grasping on to each movement, it will develop a natural and effortless calm. You will also reinforce the central aim of the handshake practice—to detach from the habit of reacting to every mental movement.

This is an effortless awareness that is present without any action on your part except to allow it to naturally happen. Invariably, you will get pulled back into mental appearances. If this becomes more than a minor disruption, it is important for you to return to the earlier techniques, calming the mind once again. If not, simply apply the nonjudgmental handshake approach. The mental appearance will dissipate on its own, leaving in its wake the open awareness. The issue is not seeking a mind without thoughts, but rather an awareness that is not distracted. You allow the mind to give rise to appearances, as it will, but you don't follow them. Maintain this simple, fully alert, and clear basic awareness until your practice time is complete. Remember, if your mind does not naturally quiet down, then it is best for you to focus on the first two exercises, leaving this approach for another time.

BASIC WELL-BEING

With practice you will be able to prolong the time you can remain in open awareness without being pulled into mental activity. Here and there you may even catch a glimpse of what is called "basic well-being." That is the experience of ease, contentment, and peace that self-exists in the natural resting place of the mind. It does not have to be created. In fact, it cannot be created; it is naturally present when the clouds of mental activity dissipate and what remains is the simple awareness of mind. Basic well-being is a place innate to all of us. It is always there. It has no reason or cause. We simply have to allow our natural self to reveal itself.

In the previous chapter, we talked about developing the capacity to lose all fear of our self—our thoughts and feelings. Here we are going further. We are not only letting go of fear and anxiety, but we are also discovering a place within us that is already and always there, a natural home that is content, peaceful, and whole. Regardless of the difficult challenges of the in-between time, we will know that there is a place of rest, refuge, and well-being within, already and at all times. To lose our old self and then find our authentic self is a great accomplishment and gift. But remember, first get the basic exercise down, and only then try meditation without support.

Integrating Practice into Daily Life

It is important to expand our capacity to bring all of daily life into our journey. So we will now add a further very important daily life practice. This is also a mindfulness practice, one that is focused on listening. It is called mindful listening. We spend much of our life listening to others. But are we really listening? Much like learning to listen to our inner self, we must similarly learn to deeply listen to others. Therefore, you will note the similarity in instructions.

Each day, choose one or more conversations for practice. Choose those that are important to you or may be somewhat difficult. They will be your greatest teachers. This is a meditation with support. The support is the other person's speaking. You focus with complete attention on their words. What will occur very soon is that you will cease listening to the other and begin to listen to your internal commentary. That break in communication may take a variety of forms. You may judge, psychologize, or otherwise interpret their communication, "zone out," or become occupied with formulating a premature response. Much as when you get distracted in the breathing exercise, you cut off these mental distractions with or without a handshake practice, and return to undistracted listening. You may have to bring yourself back to the listening again and again. But if you practice this open meditative listening, it will become quite natural in time.

If you can continue undistracted listening until the end of the conversation, you will notice something quite remarkable. First, because you are actually transforming listening into a meditation, you will experience an inner quiet and calm. Second, the other, who has been acknowledged and heard (a rare experience for all of us) will also be calm and peaceful. Third, you will feel connected to this person, and isn't that the purpose of communication? Finally, you will not have to concern yourself with the proper response. Either the listening in itself will be sufficient, the individual will tell you what they need, or you will know intuitively what to do.

The practices of resting in stillness and mindful listening will support your inner growth and serve as a resource for moving through your life transition. These are important and precious skills.

Chapter 5

STAGE FOUR:
Lessons Learned

Where then there was darkness, now there is light;
but also where light was, there now is darkness.
The modern hero-deed must be that of questing to bring
to light again the lost Atlantis of the coordinated soul.

—JOSEPH CAMPBELL, FROM *THE HERO WITH A THOUSAND FACES*

The precious and life-altering lessons learned in the in-between time are about self and life, who we are and who we are not. We've worked hard to gain the insights and wisdom that underlie our journey to a larger life. We've let go of familiar, but outdated, lifestyles and beliefs, overcome obstacles and challenges, and learned from teachers and readings. But of greatest importance is the learning gained by diving into the depths of our life where we meet, with a sense of familiarity and delight, our authentic self.

The lessons learned do not come all at once. Yes, there are some important "aha" moments, but it is the ongoing experience of the in-between time that is the master teacher. Navigating the in-between time requires time, patience, faith, and perseverance. We slowly leave the in-between time much differently than when we entered. We are wiser, more confident, and more capable of living an authentic and conscious life. Enduring life lessons are learned and sustain us as we re-create our self.

The Lesson of Humility

Like King Oedipus, one day a king and the next day a blind pauper, we discover that what separates our circumstance from that of another is no more than the brief moment between two beats of the heart. The breakdown of our customary supports leaves us bare, stripped to the core. We can no longer hide behind an exaggerated ego and its built-up identities, material acquisitions, and social status. Achievement, success, control, and security—the ceaseless efforts of the ego—cannot follow us into our transitions. The decision to move toward a larger life forces us to let go of these false gods and drops us into our simple humanity. Our transitions are about tomorrow, not yesterday. Our transitions are about authenticity and heart.

I recall the deflation that occurred in my life. Within a short period of time, I left a long-term marriage and departed my work as a physician, losing two of my major identities. One day everything fit in place, life was going well, and applause and appreciation came my way and stoked my pridefulness. The next day the paper supports fell down, and in mind and body, I was like everyone else, as I had always been, struggling to understand self and life. The transition that followed allowed me to slowly discover a deeper and natural pride that was strong and invulnerable. But, for that, I had to look within.

As we move through transition, a simple and heartfelt humility progressively takes the place of false pride. Denied the imaginings of an inflated "I," we arrive at an enduring sense of self that is inner-based, natural, and unassuming. This authentic self neither relies upon nor is propped up by external identities or experiences. It is a natural soft presence at the center of our being characterized by simple decency, honesty, compassion, and goodness—qualities that are innate to our authentic self. They are not dependent on outer circumstances. There is no pretense.

There is a sense of relief that we no longer have to carry the effort and exhaustion associated with a false self and false pride. We can just be who we are, and that is a source of humble and well-earned pride.

This natural humility breaks down the walls that separate us from others. We understand that the differences in individual circumstances are ever changing. But our shared essence is much the same. We all seek happiness and the absence of suffering, and we all experience what is common to our humanity—basic goodness, a tender vulnerability, and selfless compassion. False pride is what we create. Humility, we discover, is who we are at the center of our being. As the layers fall away, keep a watch for a natural humility to reveal itself. That is an important discovery that's gained by consciously moving through transition.

The Lesson of Change

When we enter transition, chosen or not, much of what we considered secure and solid is swept away in what seems like a moment. We are abruptly and rudely confronted with the truth of impermanence. Everything changes over time. Nothing is permanent. We know that intellectually. We accept the reality of obvious change—night alternating with day, the passing of the seasons, and to a lesser extent aging and death. Yet, in our psychological life, where change is personal and threatening, we try to keep things as they are. We do all that we can to fix them in place, freeze the natural rhythms of life, and deny the unavoidable confrontation with the truth of change.

We grasp on to people, beliefs, identities, and material possessions, as if our grasping could alter their fundamental impermanence. We want solid ground. We seek security and familiarity more than the fluidity and vitality that is life itself as it is. The in-between time forces us to see the truth of change—the fragility and impermanence of all things. It teaches us that regardless of our efforts, we cannot hold back the movement of life. It moves. It changes. It flows like a river.

Paradoxically, the recognition of the reality of impermanence simultaneously reveals the possibility of an inner security and vitality that can serve as an *unchanging* refuge in a changing world. As we develop a stable inner life, we progressively discover this inner-based stability that never leaves us and never changes. As a result, we learn to welcome outer change without fear or anxiety. At the center of our being, our authentic spark of life never changes, regardless of the impermanence of the outer world. That's true, reassuring, and liberating.

We've moved through the in-between time and survived the fears, trials, and darkness. We've tasted the vitality of new growth. We now know that letting go of outdated and exhausted approaches to life leads to renewal and revitalization. As a result, we have the capacity to move through future challenges with less fear, resistance, or procrastination. We become more comfortable at our edges and more willing to risk and seek adventure. Our lives have a much greater span than those who turn away from life's challenges. Change becomes a friend that allows us to intermittently refresh our life and bring it in alignment with new and changing realities. Our frozen winter has given way to spring.

As a result of the lesson of impermanence, our life progressively gains fluidity, exuberance, and vitality. We're increasingly comfortable and trustful of its natural unfolding, and even somewhat curious to see what is next.

The Lesson of Listening

Why is the practice of meditation so essential to transition? It is because meditation teaches us how to listen to our self, to the deeper wisdom of our inner life. Listening deeply, fully, and with an "open" and impartial mind requires mental spaciousness free of mind chatter. The overactive mind is like a fish aquarium filled with silt. We cannot see through to the other side. We cannot see clearly. But, when the silt settles to the bottom, there is clarity. Then we can see.

It's like that with listening to our self. When the overactive mind settles, we can finally listen to the insights and wisdom that speak to us with truth and authenticity. That knowledge is already and always with us, but we cannot hear it through the noise of the everyday mind. We cannot hear it through our habitual perceptions and reactions. The capacity to hear one's wisdom and truth is the reason why it's so important to train and tame the mind through meditative practice and settle into the mind's natural silence and stillness.

Listening, as I speak of it here, is listening free of our usual thoughts, opinions, judgments, likes and dislikes, or those of others. When we listen through our cognitive process, we only hear another version of our past history. We cannot hear what is below and came before our acquired ideas and false self. For this we need to clear the mind, rest in stillness and silence, and allow the authentic reality of our self and life to emerge and inform us. Unless we slow our life, diminish self-sabotaging busyness, sit still, and let go of our overactive mind, we cannot hear the vital messages from below, messages that will guide our transition and stamp it with authenticity and truth.

Learning to listen to our depths and trust its voice is of great value before, during, and after transition. Before a transition, listening to our inner voice can inform us that our outer life is not in balance with our nature. In the middle of transition, listening provides us access to inner stillness and inner truth. After transition, listening allows us to continuously monitor the ongoing experience of our life.

The Lesson of the Present Moment

We live through fixed ways of perceiving experience and habitual response patterns. Their origin is past experience. Although it may seem otherwise, we rarely live in the present moment. But now we have a choice. When the strong pull of the past has dropped away and the future remains largely unknown, there is nothing but the present moment. That is all we can live in. There is a strange relief in being forced to live moment to moment. Gone with the past are our fears and anxieties. There is no longer anything to gain or lose. We can dance carefree in what is as is.

What are the lessons learned by this forced embrace of the present moment? We discover that there is a freshness and vividness that is not experienced when we shape our current experience through past conditioning. There is fluidity, a spontaneous flow of life. There is a growing sense of life as naked, raw, and unfiltered by memory. There may be intimations of a lost child-like awe, wonder, and curiosity. It is called a "beginner's mind."

Life also slows down. Because there is no specific agenda in the in-between time, there is no place to go and no urgency. We live what is there in the moment and can "hang out" with it until the next moment. We discover a certain ease, freedom, and delight. During this brief parenthesis in life, we don't have to do anything or be anyplace. I don't want to suggest that life, during this period, is all sweet and cheery. It isn't. The moments of insight, the lessons learned, and an increasing lightness of being will still alternate with moments of darkness and confusion. The good news is that the latter will diminish and the former will become more stable.

We can listen to the end of a conversation, linger with a meal, enjoy a sunset, read, relax, and just be at ease. Instead of controlling life, we are letting go and allowing it to unfold by itself, moment to moment. By being with our experience as it is happening, we discover that there is a natural resolution to issues and challenges that previously consumed endless mental energy. Life is not as complex as it seems. Living in the moment brings with it a certain sense of carefree simplicity, an experience of life that we will want to integrate into life ahead.

There is also an intangible sense of aliveness in the now. The more fully we live in the moment, the greater the sense of that aliveness. There are no fireworks that announce our forced arrival in the now. It seems ordinary, simple, free, and flowing. At the time, there isn't much of an alternative.

The "unchosen" experience of living in the moment is an important life lesson. It will continue to serve us well, as we return to day-to-day life.

The Lesson of Trust

As we move through the challenges of transition, we discover an inner source of guidance and well-being that feels natural and reliable. We make the remarkable discovery that there is a place in each of us, a deeper self accessed in the stillness of the mind that knows who we are and the unique character of our life. That knowledge is pristine. It predates our personal life experience. It is the wisdom of our soul, our essence. We can trust it.

It is not as easy as looking up information on the computer. We have to access this wisdom by going inward, sitting still over and over, and listening carefully without an agenda. We cannot rush the process. It unfolds only when we have the patience to wait. Any grasping, pushing, or urgency stops forward movement. When we are ready, when we are ripe, the doors will open and the answers will arise by themselves. The poet Rainer Rilke expresses it in the following words in *Letters to a Young Poet:*

Be patient toward all that is unsolved in your heart and try to love the questions themselves, like locked rooms and like books that are now written in a very foreign tongue. Do not now seek the answers, which cannot be given you because you would not be able to live them. And the point is, to live everything. Live the questions now. Perhaps you will then gradually, without noticing it, live along some distant day into the answer.

That is how it works for all of us. Be patient, allow the space for your inner knowing to express itself, and trust that the answers you seek will naturally reveal themselves. The capacity for inner knowing and the ability for it to express itself in its own way and in its own time is what you are learning to trust. Trust your authentic self.

As we progressively gain insight and understanding, we simultaneously gain confidence in our capacity to navigate life in accordance with our essential nature. It is not like the confidence that comes from practicing something over and over, like a pianist or carpenter. It is a confidence that comes from the increasing recognition that we have the know-how to orchestrate our lives from within. We know we will be okay. That kind of confidence is a trust in life itself. We trust that it will give us what we need when we need it, and when we momentarily lose our way, we know that we can tune in once again and listen deeply to the clarity and truth of our inner wisdom.

A conscious transition teaches us to have confidence and trust in our self. We no longer need to reach out for an outer fix. We know that our wisdom lies within and that when cultivated with a still mind and quiet listening, it will naturally emerge to inform our life.

The Lesson of Surrender

We do not choose surrender. We are forced into it. When all has fallen away as we enter the groundlessness and confusion of the in-between time, our usual ways of controlling life no longer work. And that's very difficult to digest. Our little self has run out of its ways of bending life to its desires, preferences, and needs. We are out of control, and there is nothing we can do about it except to acknowledge and learn from it.

I well remember this time in my own life. The in-between time allowed me, or perhaps I should say forced me, to stumble upon a basic truth. My little "I" never really controlled anything. Its small seeming successes, here and there, were a mere illusion. In the greater scheme of life, I couldn't control loss, disease, aging, death, others, or most of the annoying adversities and challenges of life. And, I realized, it's exhausting to mind, body, and spirit to attempt, much less to persist, in this impossible effort.

What's required is an acknowledgment and surrender to the reality of the here and now, even if that is a painful reality. We must surrender the illusion that we can control life and thus avoid or minimize loss. We must surrender the willful belief that life should proceed according to our desires and preferences. And we must surrender the seductive illusion that life and its circumstances are unchanging. Letting go of our resistance is not a punishment. It is a wise act of courage that allows an easier passage through loss as well as an openness to possibilities as yet unknown.

And, if are truly fortunate, something further may happen. In the sadness and pain, the heart's vulnerability and tenderness can be felt. If we rest into that vulnerability of confusion and groundlessness without judgment or reaction, we may find a place of peace and sustenance. Yes, in the center of the full experience of distress, there is spaciousness and peace.

As we walk through life's adversities and challenges with wisdom, grace, and surrender, there is something very important waiting to greet us. The pain of the confusion and disorientation progressively burn away our little self and its illusion of control. We increasingly become *free* of our stories, fears, anxieties, and ceaseless mental commentaries.

What we learn from surrender is the silliness of our efforts to control the great movements of life, and the inevitable freedom and possibility that arise as we flow with life, rather than oppose it. Forced to surrender during the in-between time, we discover that surrender is a virtue to cultivate throughout our life.

The Lesson of Authenticity

We usually know and measure ourselves by our roles: physician, father, lover, sister, fixer, activist, and so on. That is who we are, or at least that is who we think we are. At the depths, we learn about another self, one that does not as easily lend itself to labels, categories, and job descriptions. It is subtler. Although it cannot be known through the senses, those who have experienced this aspect of self know it to be far more authentic and enduring.

Our former self now appears more like a social mask, a constructed persona. It may serve a purpose in living life, but it is best that we don't mistake it for who we are at our center. That deeper self is steady, unchanging, and invulnerable. To discover it feels like finally returning home. Consider the words of the poet Derek Walcott in "Love After Love":

> The time will come
> when, with elation,
> you will greet yourself arriving
> at your own door, in your own mirror,
> and each will smile at the other's welcome.

Your inner authentic self will smile at your outer acquired self. As the poet continues, "… give back your heart to itself, to the stranger that has loved you all of your life, whom you ignored for another, who knows you by heart."

That is why it is essential, when we enter transition, to divest ourselves of *attachment* to our usual identities. Only when our masks and personas can be put aside for a moment can we see our original face, can we greet our self, arriving at our own door.

Our authentic self offers a strong, secure, and unchanging foundation upon which we can build a revitalized life. With this self-knowledge, we can define our values from the inside, values that are in accord with our nature rather than past experience or social imperatives.

Of course we will still assume roles and identities with which we live daily life. But these will neither be mistaken as our essential self nor will they be inconsistent with our authentic nature.

There is a wise and skillful dance we learn to do, a dance between our inner and outer life. We become a master of two worlds. We learn how to skillfully express our authenticity in the practicalities of daily living. There is no requirement that there be tension between the two.

With time we learn to know and hold our center, spreading it outward to embrace all of our life. Our authentic self becomes the hub of our life with varying identities emerging from this hub to meet the needs of daily life, and then returning to be reformed into new identities as needed. Our inner and outer life becomes a seamless unified experience. That is the lesson of authenticity.

The treacherous and difficult passage through the in-between time eventually comes to its end, even as its lessons continue to be learned and integrated into one's life. These heart lessons, and that is what I will call them, are the gift of transition. They are the essential skills and capacities required for a healthy human life that flourishes over time.

Heart Advice from a Fellow Traveler

1. The great myths and stories help us to recognize parts of ourselves that are otherwise hidden from view. Through the particulars of myth and story, we come to know that our journey is one that calls every individual. Our journey of awakening is not ours alone. It is part of a larger drama, a universal human experience. Many have preceded us through the stages of transition. Their pain, struggle, and triumph are our pain, struggle, and triumph. We are not alone in our transitions.

2. With the above in mind, I would like to share a personal story. As I have mentioned before, each of us who departs on the journey of transition will discover that the first passage is the most difficult and transforming. That is the way it was for me. My in-between time lasted almost nine months. During this period, my experiences and lessons learned were much as I've described in this and previous chapters. What I would like to share with you now is the moment in which the shape-shifting realization took place, the epiphany experienced, the moment of self-discovery revealed.

For many months I had been wandering in the in-between time, in the very difficult nothingness that is marked by confusion and, at times, despair. I had finally reached a point at which nothing seemed to matter anymore. I felt hopelessly lost in an abyss, unable to return to where I had come from and unable to move forward. And although I had a steadfast faith in the process, I felt both motionless and powerless. I recall remarking to a friend, " I could eat a peanut butter sandwich or jump off a building. In many ways it would seem much the same." Such was the darkness that enveloped my life at the pinnacle of the in-between time.

At a friend's suggestion, I scheduled an appointment with a

psychologist whose spiritual capacities were no less than his psychological skills. I was skeptical that anything could help, but then again, there wasn't much to lose. I drove to his office in downtown Washington on a typically hot and humid summer day. He greeted me with kindness and pointed to a seat on a couch a few feet away from his chair. He asked me to tell him about my situation.

Barely waiting for me to complete my tale, he asked me to close my eyes. "What are you feeling?" he said. "Nothing," I replied, "Absolutely nothing." "Make an image of that," he said. I did. He next asked me to describe the image. I replied, "It's a big hollow sphere." "Are you in or near it?" he inquired. "Yes," I said, "I'm in the inside of it." "How big are you?" "Quite small," I answered." He then asked me to make myself disappear from my image, an act of the imagination that given my circumstance was not very difficult to do. "What's left?" he asked, "Nothing," I answered. And then he said four words that will forever remain etched in my heart and mind: "That's who you are." In no more than the moment between two beats of the heart, my understanding entirely changed.

In a timeless silence, I found what I had been searching for. As I wrote in my journal later that day, " . . . stripped of all my supports, stripped of my hopes and fears, self-imposed restraints, stripped of my beliefs and ideas—my rights, wrongs, shoulds, shouldn'ts, goods, bads, affirmations, and rejections—I finally found my self, a very different self, in the inner emptiness that suddenly and remarkably seemed filled with abundance." As I sat in that office, tears began to flow, the kind of tears that only come with the ecstasy that accompanies a numinous experience, a sacred epiphany.

No more than twenty minutes of our scheduled hour had passed, and yet I knew with clarity and certainty that I had touched truth. Although the breakthrough was instantaneous, the incubation of the in-between time had been essential. Confusion and despair gave way to a lighthearted joy. There was a strange combination of feelings: pride that I had risked all and stayed the course, gratefulness for the gift of life, awe at the magnificence of the deeper mysteries, and a strange sadness and sense of loss that came with the recognition that I was about to leave the difficult, intense, and yet very alive and fertile alive moments I had spent in the in-between time.

At the end of the session, the psychologist suggested that I go away to a retreat site for a few weeks of rest, reflection, and consideration of my new life. I left the next day. When I headed home two weeks later, I was ready to return to *my* life, the next stage of transition.

3. The lessons learned in transition will grow and evolve over many years. They will deepen in understanding and be progressively integrated into daily life. The in-between time gives way to the next stage, the return.

EXERCISE #4: THE WISDOM OF THE MIND

Intellectual knowledge arises from one aspect of mind. Wisdom arises from a very different aspect. Intellectual understanding is a cognitive descriptive knowledge. It is a form of "book learning." It is quite valuable in living day-to-day life. At its most refined stage it is the realm of the sage. However, thought and intellect cannot fully inform us about the fundamental truths of life, our own life included. Knowledge that arises from personal experience is noncognitive, nonintellectual knowledge. It is precise, accurate, and complete. When it comes to knowing the depths of life, direct knowledge is necessary. That is the realm of the spiritual being.

To know the essential truths that will guide an authentic life, we must go beyond the intellect and allow the noncognitive aspect of mind to reveal itself. This does not mean we discard intellect, but rather, we reserve it for what it does best—living out our choices in day-to-day-life. The challenge of a life transition opens a crack in the well-ordered structure of our life and lets new understandings reveal themselves.

The question is, how do we intentionally access this aspect of mind to reveal the deeper lessons of life? You've already begun that process through the practices discussed. Calming the mind removes the clouds of mental noise that obscures noncognitive knowledge. When we further incorporate the handshake meditation, we remove the obstacle associated with struggling, suppressing, or repressing mental movements. We let go and let be. Finally, when we rest in stillness, we stabilize the natural resting place of the mind. It is from this fertile ground that insight, wisdom, and the deeper qualities of human life arise.

Calming the mind and relating in a positive and liberating way to mental chatter don't have to wait forever. Here and there, when the gap spontaneously opens, and one's mind rests in stillness, there may arise a sudden and unexpected truth that is life altering. We call this an "aha" experience. Usually, they are serendipitous; however, with meditation practice, we cultivate the ground from which they arise. When you touch into an authentic and life-altering insight, associated insights will rapidly fall into place. You will discover this for yourself.

We encourage this process so that we can extend and expand the lessons learned during transition. We accomplish this by continuing to cultivate through practice the natural still resting place of the mind. We don't aim for insights. We just cultivate the soil. If your mind remains still and undistracted for periods of time, you have taken an important step to "encourage" the stability and function of the noncognitive mind.

The Practice

When, during a practice session, your mind has some stability of stillness and silence, you may offer a very subtle and undemanding intention. If there is a particular issue you are concerned about, briefly expose your still mind to that issue. It may be a work, relationship, or a general life issue. Whatever the nature of your concern, it is important to be clear, simple, and brief. Do not activate the thinking mind by posing a complex question.

Next, place that question in the background of your mind and return to resting in stillness, holding a very subtle sense of the question asked. Remain in stillness, "handshaking" and letting go of any distractions that arise, as you have done before. If the time is right, clarity may arise and a deeper understanding may emerge. That is related to the level of mental stability, the ease through which you let the process proceed, and the development of clarity.

Let me share some thoughts about mental clarity. Usually the mind is unclear. It is obscured by random mental "noise." Remember the metaphor we used before? A fish aquarium filled with silt lacks clarity. You cannot see through it to the other side. When the silt settles, there the clarity is. Of course it was always there. It was just obscured by the silt. Similarly, when the obscuring noise of the mind calms down, the mind becomes clear. There is no obscuring veil that hides inner knowing. So, first, we develop clarity by calming the mind, and then we expand its stability and spaciousness. It is this stable and spacious clarity that transforms into the all-important insights. The mind's transparency allows the deeper truths to become evident. We directly "taste" the truths of our mind by joining with them. That is the source of all authentic knowledge.

When you have completed this process, return to resting in stillness or mindful breathing. Perhaps this is the time you will gain an insight, perhaps not. In any case, you will be cultivating the soil, which greatly increases the probability of experience important noncognitive insights. When your practice session is complete, return to the time and space of your room.

Integrating Practice into Daily Life

Let's now shift to another daily practice, adding it to your expanding repertoire. Remember, in modern life we live in the world, in the marketplace rather than in a seminary or monastery. As a result, we must learn to use the activities of daily life as teachers and opportunities to extend the learning that comes with transition. I have already mentioned the process of flashing back to the inner space of meditation during the day, practicing mindfulness with one's daily activities and practicing mindful listening. I would now like to add a more general, but very important, practice—transforming one's daily challenges into learning opportunities.

While the focus of this book is to guide you through the stages of a life transition, there are smaller challenges that you confront each day. The exercise here is to observe how you approach these challenges. Do you get annoyed, angry, point a finger, feel victimized, anxious, or moody? Just observe with a neutral viewpoint, as if you were a journalist watching an event. Identify your style.

Next, try to approach each challenging circumstance as a teaching opportunity. Rather than seeking who is to blame, consider how you can learn from this circumstance. How can you transform seeming adversity into opportunity? We all know the stories of famous individuals who have done just that. They have met adversity and grown from it. Consider Nelson Mandela's years in prison, Viktor Frankl's experience in a concentration camp, or Tibetan monks in detention centers. In each case, adversity enhanced mental health rather, than destroyed it. The same is true for many unknown individuals who also transform adversity into a cause for growth.

In this exercise, imagine that there are two responses to adversity. One is to collapse into blame, anger, and despair, and the other is to skillfully use that circumstance to learn and grow. Take a difficult situation and see the result of a shift in attitude and approach. If this is difficult, get some space, practice a bit of meditation, and then reconsider how to handle the circumstance. Each experience can be a mini-transition, a mini-breakthrough.

Chapter 6

STAGE FIVE:
The Return

The world stands out on either side
No wider than the heart is wide;
Above the world is stretched the sky, —
No higher than the soul is high.

—EDNA ST. VINCENT MILLAY, FROM "RENASCENCE"

The experiences and lessons learned in the in-between time must be brought back and integrated into daily life. We've learned how to adventure into uncharted territories, live in the moment, listen deeply, trust life, and access an ever-present inner source of well-being. We have gained confidence, competence, and wisdom. We've answered the call, traversed the in-between time, and found our way to the light. And that light opens a world that is increasingly boundless.

There is an understandable reluctance to return to day-to-day life. The ancient Hindu Upanishads ask, "Who having cast off the world would desire to return again?" It is a question we will surely ask ourselves. We have had a numinous experience, perhaps an ecstatic one, and a taste of freedom. We have cast off outdated shackles, touched sacred mysteries, discovered essential truths, and recognized the limitations of a surface existence. Finally, at the very moment we are ready to cross back into society, life seems complete and peaceful. So why take the next step?

In fact, some don't. They refuse to return, preferring to live in that second Garden of Eden. They choose to live a monastic life, either as part of an organized religious community or in a self-designed retreat to a simpler life on the edges of society. In Jungian terms, they have been captured by an archetype, a singular, enchanting, and compelling vision of life.

But most us living in modern times will hear society beckon. Just as we are called to transition, we will be called back to day-to-day life—family, relationships, work, and service. In *The Hero with a Thousand Faces,* Joseph Campbell says, "Society is jealous of those who remain away from it, and will come knocking at the door."

As we exit the in-between time, we use the lessons learned to revitalize day-to-day life. In actuality, solitude, contemplation, living in the moment, the touchstone of a deeper self, personal authenticity, and wisdom are the ground of a healthy human life. The challenge is to infuse day-to-day life and society with what we have gained in transition. We return as healers to the awaiting world.

Reentry

Reentry into day-to-day life can be a cultural shock. Having learned the value of silence, we return to a cacophony of sound; having seen the essential truths, we return to a world of confusion; having stripped away false pretenses, we return to a society that's all dressed up; having lived a slow and deliberate pace, we return to fast-paced materialistic lifestyles; and having moved through the solitude of the in-between time, we are now with friends and family who may neither understand where we have been nor comprehend our transition. It may not be that dramatic, but it is likely that you will feel some sense of "cultural shock."

The challenge of reentry is the perception that we must give up our newly discovered world of depth and dimension for a day-to-day world that now seems somewhat superficial and transitory. Ordinary life, seen from the perspective of the inner life, may at first seem a difficult pill to swallow. Our initial task must be to resolve this challenge.

I have already alluded to one potential resolution. Before we began our transition, we firmly believed that the world we lived in, the world of daily life, was the only existing universe. We thought our day-to-day experience was the full extent of life. When we pass through the in-between time, we discover another world that underlies and gives dimension to day-to-day life—our discovery of that rich inner world doesn't invalidate the outer world. It merely places it in a larger context. The outer world becomes part of our experience, not all of it. Daily life becomes part of a larger whole.

There is a story in the East about a monk who perpetually complains to his teacher about the rigors and distress of his path. The teacher asks him to place a half-cup of salt in a glass of water and drink it. When he asks the monk how it tastes, the young man replies, "Very bitter." Next, the teacher asks him to take that same amount of salt and drop it into a lake. When the monk does as requested, the teacher instructs him to take a drink of the lake water. "Now, how did *that* taste?" the teacher asks. "Fresh," the student responds. "Then, it must not be the salt that is the problem," says the teacher, "but rather, the container in which it is held."

On our return to daily life, we begin to hold it in a far larger container of understanding—the container of a larger self rather than a smaller self. We comprehend that mental distress and suffering are not merely personal issues, but rather, human ones. That understanding dilutes our personal sense of alienation and grief. We have also found within an immutable container of serenity and contentment that can hold the challenges and difficulties of human life. We have seen through to the more essential truths that shed light and goodness on all of our experiences. Like the student monk, we have discovered that distress and suffering is relative to the quality of the container it is held in. As we grow in "size" and "dimension," distress and suffering diminish and eventually dissipate.

The psychologist C.G. Jung stated that the aim of a fully lived life is to first *spiritualize the material* and then return to *materialize the spirit*. First, we must leave the world to explore the depths and authenticity of our life, spiritualizing the material. Then, we return to integrate that knowledge into our daily experiences, materializing the spirit. In Christianity, this double movement first reaches toward the divine and is then followed by the return to worldly bearing the gift of compassion, agape. The Yogi philosopher Aurobindo termed these two movements the ascent and descent. In the Buddhist tradition, they are termed wisdom and compassion. The message is the same. It's a universal one. We leave our outdated lives to discover greater meaning and return as healers to the world and our planet.

New Values

As we leave the in-between time, we start the process of easing in and taking care to hold our center as we rejoin day-to-day life. We choose the values that will guide our life, the shape of our new identity, and the actions we will take. We learn to integrate inner authenticity into outer life. We remain aligned with our inner life, as we navigate the outer world.

Family, teachers, and culture imposed on us the values and perspectives that guided our earlier life. We did not choose them and were unable, as a result of our youth, to question their appropriateness in our life. Guided by these "acquired" values and beliefs, our life unfolded. We established an identity, chose a career, and established relationships. When our outer life felt inconsistent with our natural tendencies and temperaments, we experienced confusion, anxiety, and doubt. That's how an inauthentic life shows up over time. Transition is the medicine that offers us the opportunity to let go of these inherited values, find our own truth, and live them in a revitalized daily life.

As a trained physician, I slowly discovered that the values and beliefs assimilated from my medical training were at odds with how I saw my life as a healer. I discovered that conventional medicine and its exclusive emphasis on the physical aspects of health was not right for me. It was not aligned with my core values. My concern was with well-being rather than disease, self-reliance rather than dependency, and self-development and human flourishing in contrast to a mere disease-free "normality." By letting go of what was not me and discovering my own values, I was able to reenter the stream of medical practice with a new perspective, direction, and passion. I could accept the brilliance and value of scientific medicine, but within a much larger container.

Ann, who you met in the first chapter, found it important to stop relying on her parents and surrogate parent, her husband. It was critical that she learn to live alone, to trust in her ability to care, decide, and act for herself. It became valuable for her to say yes when she meant yes and no when she meant no. Richard, who you also met in the first chapter, found that his values were shifting. His single-minded goal of professional achievement no longer seemed to be the priority it once was. The energy he previously poured into his career was transferred to new priorities. He chose to simplify his life, play, be more intimate and expressive with his wife and children, and invest in some of his long-forgotten dreams.

As you allow yourself time and spaciousness, the next step will slowly reveal itself. You don't have to work for it as much as be receptive. A hint, a new idea, a dream, or a particular image will surface. Remember how it happened to John. He asked why a patient was late for his office appointment. The answer for John, something another person may have given little attention, became the basis for a new personal ideal. For Jennifer, the hint came in the form of an imaginary eagle emerging from her chest. Be patient, begin to live, try one thing and then another, and all the time listen carefully. It is not important how long it takes, but rather that when it arrives, it is authentically you.

But don't expect your new priorities to jump right out at you. They won't. Remember the poet Rilke's admonition to "love the questions." Don't be misled into thinking that everything from the past must be left in the past. Some of the values you previously held may have been right for you. The idea is to consider them carefully, and then choose for yourself.

Shifting Identities

Before we entered the in-between time, we had an unchanging sense of ourselves, a singular fixed identity and self-image. We didn't know we were wearing a mask, living a persona given to us by others. We mistook it for who we were. But, returning from the in-between time, we know much more about ourselves. We've discovered a deeper, more authentic self, one that has a more fluid sense of specific identity. There is my deepest authentic self, and then there are the changing outer identities. From the perspective of this newly discovered center of our existence, we realize that our social identities are what we create and play with in the outer world. They define what we do and assist us in navigating daily life. They are not who we are.

No longer compelled to live out our acquired identity, we now have many choices. Our life on the outside can be expressed in a variety of forms that shift and change according to our circumstances. Moist clay in the potter's hand can become a pot, vase, or any other shape, and then return to its moist formlessness. However, the essence of clay always remains the same, whatever shape it takes. Similarly, whatever the shape or form of a wave, the ocean is always present in the wave. Whatever identity we create, our authentic essence is unchanging and inseparable from its outer form. Our outer identities come and go. The only immutable self is found in the formless constancy of the essential self, from which all of our social identities arise and eventually return.

We can be a solid citizen or a wanderer, a parent, a lover, a healer, an artist, a craftsman, or any other possibility or combination. Perhaps we shall be one identity during the week and another on weekends, one in the fall and another in the spring. Think of the dynamism that life takes on when we allow for our full repertoire of possibilities. There is a time for each. Being a lover at work can cause great difficulty, but being a worker at home can create much the same difficulty. There are years during which we may choose to fully develop one identity and give the others less priority and other times when we will want to use all of them. We have infinite possibilities. We are polychromatic.

When I reentered day-to-day life, it surprised me that I decided to return to my role as a physician, to once more accept that identity. However, there was one critical difference. I found that I could accept the role of scientist/physician much as I had learned it, as long as I could expand it to include a larger set of values. I choose to look beyond the singular approach to healing taught in medical training. I chose to consider other approaches, to disregard the so-called clinical distance that separated me from my clients, to see symptoms in a broader context, and to redefine my previously limited ideas about health. I assumed a new identity as a physician.

However we choose to create and live our outer identities, it is crucial to remain in touch with the unchanging self that underlies them. It is our anchor, our compass, our essential self. We will meet it whenever we are sufficiently silent. When we lose this contact, we will once again get lost in the outer world. We will forget who we are. We will mistakenly become our identities. Our outer life is authentic when it is in direct relationship with the center of our being; otherwise, it is disconnected from our essential self. Take your time, play with your identities, and be serious about life—all in the same moment.

Conscious Action

Day-to-day living requires action. Previously, our actions could more aptly be called reactions. Automatically, in accordance with learned habitual patterns, we responded predictably to life's circumstances. However, the Yogis taught us about another type of action. They believed that actions don't have to be driven by past history. They can arise from an accurate intuited sense of what the present moment calls for. That is what they termed "conscious action"—one that's in complete accord with our immediate experience. It's a response that is not filtered through past perspectives and habitual reactive patterns.

Our response to a life circumstance is most often shaped by unconscious mental patterns. These patterns unfold automatically, determining our emotional and physical response. These actions accord more with our past than with the actual circumstance of the present moment. That's why our customary actions are called reactions. They are formulated and shaped in accordance with fixed perceptions and habitual patterns stored in memory. In contrast, a conscious action spontaneously arises from the basic goodness at the center of our being.

Consider the actions of a mother when her child suddenly falls into the water. Does she think about it? Does she respond from a learned pattern? Obviously not. Without thought or reliance on habitual patterns, she naturally jumps in to rescue her drowning child. That's what is meant by an action that is precisely in accord with the circumstance. Getting out of the way of an approaching car, caring for a loved one who suddenly falls ill, the innate desire to respond to suffering, and random acts of kindness are further examples. Observe your own actions. Notice actions that seem to naturally unfold in relationship to the circumstance. Notice when there is a feeling of flow. Also notice when your actions get caught up in a patterned response that never feels quite right. In time, you will be able to discern the difference between a reaction and a natural action.

Selfless Action

There is another aspect of our actions that should also be considered. As we grow through transition, our heart softens and begins to move away from exclusively ego-centered motivations. We cease to calculate and measure our actions based solely on how they may benefit our own life. Having traversed a life transition, we have a better understanding of the human condition. We know suffering. We know fear. We know that others suffer much as we do and want happiness no less than ourselves. We slowly begin to act from a different motivation, a more noble and expansive motivation. Rather than always seeking to benefit our self—gain more security, collect greater wealth, praise, and name—we reorient our self toward a concern for the welfare of others.

We are increasingly guided by both the intention that our actions be *consistent with our nature* and *selfless in direction*. Stated another way, our concern should be for the clarity, authenticity, and selflessness of our actions. The Dali Lama calls this "intelligent self-cherishing." The more we consider others, the happier we will be in mind and heart. Here are the words of the Buddhist sage Śāntideva:

All the happiness there is in this world
Arises from wishing others to be happy,
And all the suffering there is in this world
Arises from wishing ourself to be happy.

Embracing the view of *conscious* and *selfless* action, let's now examine how we can integrate these intentions into daily life. Consider work and relationships. What yoga teaches us about work is that it must be an expression of both our natural capacities and our intention to benefit others. Traversing a life transition brings us closer to our authentic self, our natural capacities, and our unique disposition. As you grow closer to your authentic self, it is important to take an inventory of what is most natural to you, what is most in accord with your soul. It may take time for you to find precisely the right work, but that's okay. It's possible to take your current work, whatever it may be, and use it to advance your transition.

If your current work allows you the time to explore your life or complete your transition, then that is what you should be doing at the moment. If it challenges and teaches you to be less reactive, less judgmental, and more accepting of life and others, it has meaning. You can practice approaching work, any type of work, with elegance, grace, attention, and loving-kindness. Take each human interaction, irrespective of the character of your work, as an opportunity to convey calm, kindness, and healing. And as you are transforming your current work through your heartfelt actions, you can simultaneously grow into the moment in which your life's work will fully reveal itself.

Relationships can be another concern. Returning to day-to-day life you may discover that a change in values and perspectives is reflected in your choice of relationships. Once fully satisfied with living on the surface, you'll likely want more of an in-depth experience. Communication at all levels—intellectual, emotional, and spiritual—will assume greater importance. You may have fewer relationships, but they will be deeper and richer.

Relationships based on your old identity may lose their energy. Consider codependent relationships. Codependent relationships require two dependent people. When one person becomes more autonomous, the other is usually confused and perhaps even angry. Such relationships will either grow or die.

Relationships that were based on pleasing behavior—saying yes when you meant no—will also change. People who have gravitated toward you because of your willingness to fill their unmet needs or your tendency to play chameleon and mold yourself to their contours will fall away, and perhaps even point a finger and say, "What happened to you? You've changed. I don't know who you are anymore." The choice will be to grow together or withdraw.

Too often we don't learn how to develop and sustain healthy relationships. As a result, we have to study and practice the art of relationship. The poet Rainer Rilke said it this way in *Letters to a Young Poet*, "For one human being to love another: that is perhaps the most difficult of all our tasks, the ultimate, the last test and proof, the work for which all other work is but preparation."

Moving consciously through a life transition is an important part of that preparation. When we engage relationships with an inner sense of well-being, they will no longer be "sticky." They will be increasingly free of attachment, clinging, expectation, and drama. We look toward others with an open, undemanding heart to share personal growth and explore the depths and fullness of the human connection.

In each of our daily activities, conscious and selfless action progressively replaces mindless reaction. The former support inner peace and happiness, while the latter leads to suffering.

Holding the Center

For our ancestors, survival was a daily struggle. Inner development was an unknown luxury. As a result, our mind and body learned to prioritize safety and survival. Although we now have greater access to our consciousness, along with the time and capacity to develop its potential, our mind and body persist in acting in ways that are survival oriented. As a result, it is easy to forget the wisdom gained through our inner journey and fall back into old ways of thinking and living. The outer world with all its activities, intensity, and challenges can quickly seduce our mind, distracting us from our newly gained inner life.

To protect our new life, we must remain vigilant and continue to grow. We must ask and re-ask the important question, "How can I hold the center, my inner life, with its insight and wisdom, while I live in the day-to-day world? How can I infuse my daily life with the knowledge gained in the in-between time? How can I reconcile what seems like the contradictory directions of the inner and outer aspects of my life?" We will ask these questions, not once, but many times.

Holding and stabilizing your inner life requires daily attention. For this to happen, it's essential to visit with your inner world each day. The best approach is to develop a meditation technique that can serve as a bridge between the two worlds, help to quiet your mind, open the doorway to your inner experience, and provide perspective to your daily life. In the stillness of heart and mind, you will reexperience your deeper self and once again see the world from the inside out, much as you did during the in-between time. That is your time for reflection and revitalization.

?It is essential to remember that bridging both worlds is a way of life, a form of personal mastery. Our sitting meditation practice cannot be an oasis of relaxation, rest, or escape from day-to-day life. Mindfulness of our moment-to-moment experiences, meditative listening to others, conscious relationships, open-heartedness, selfless service, and kindness are day-to-day practices that support and seamlessly interweave inner and outer life.

We must slowly learn to know the feeling of being inside, being outside, and being in balance. When we are too far off in one or another direction, we can draw upon our resources—supportive friends, reading, solitude, meditation, nature, art, or movement—to rebalance our lives. Slowly, as we reconfigure ourselves through our transitions, holding our center will become easier and more natural. Just as our minds and bodies have evolved to attend first to survival, we can infuse our mind and activities with a broader view of what it means to survive and *flourish*.

Polygenesis

The ancient Greeks had a word for the process of transition. They called it "polygenesis," continuous rebirthing. Isn't that the way it should be—each day, each moment, a new experience and a new movement into life? It seems that our major transitions prepare us for a life of ongoing transition and transformation. I used to say that this or that transition lasted this or that number of years. I kept on increasing the number of years until I realized that *it's all a transition*. There is always growth and change, at times dramatic and at times less so.

As you return to day-to-day life, matured and expanded by your life transition, you will feel the tenderness and vulnerability of new growth. It is important to honor and care for this new-found authenticity and freedom. Surround yourself with individuals, groups, and environments that support and help you to cultivate your revitalized life. In time, these new beginnings will gain strength and durability. Be gentle and patient with yourself.

Heart Advice from a Fellow Traveler

1. There are major transitions and lesser ones. By describing the six major stages of a life transition, I am offering a time-tested guide to successfully navigating these precious moments in life. There are times when letting go of a dysfunctional relationship, an unsatisfying job, psychological baggage, or inappropriate expectations may take you through one or more of these stages without the intensity of a major transition. Whatever shape or form your transition may take, keep the stages of transition in mind. It will help orient your experience.

2. Remember, you still have a past. It's stored in memory. You do not need to fully discard the past. Rather, you can strip away its power to influence your life in directions that are not consciously chosen. The Yogis say that with consciousness and wisdom these old patterns remain in memory, but they remain as parched seeds that can no longer germinate and drive your life.

There are parts of your past that you will choose to leave as ancient history, as parched seeds in a remote part of memory. There are other aspects of the past that you may choose to integrate into your new life *on your own terms.* Consider all of your earlier experiences as if they were deposits in a resource bank, resources that you can draw upon whenever they fit the need of the moment. You have many resources, old and new. Choose wisely among them as you return to day-to-day life. Astute discernment will protect you from once again collecting beliefs and actions that do not fit who you are.

3. As you return to your revitalized life, take things step by step. It is unlikely that your life will suddenly appear in its "perfected form." Wisely and patiently explore new directions, learning and growing from each step. There will be forward steps, back steps, and side steps. It is all part of the process, part of the natural rhythm and unfolding of life. That's what makes it exciting and filled with adventure, curiosity, and vitality.

If you get discouraged, retreat into a few days of quiet, read some of the great stories, review the stages described in this book, and talk with friends who understand your journey. It would be silly for an acorn to insist that it become an oak in one day. Nature has its way and its seasons. Don't miss the trip by focusing on the destination. Life is living each moment authentically, not in arriving at some fixed destination.

4. It has always seemed strange to me that helpers, in one form or another, always seem to appear at the critical times. I have come to realize that when I am clear about what I need, the precise resources usually present themselves in a timely manner. Sometimes they are teachers, friends, or colleagues, and at other times an apartment, a job, or a needed source of income. Be patient. Trust life. Help is likely on the way. It usually appears at the least expected, but most appropriate, moments.

I am reminded of the great journey of Homer's Odysseus. Throughout all of his trials the goddess Athena watched over him. Only at the end of his journey did she reveal herself. But whenever he ran into trouble, she was silently at his side helping him—gently guiding his way. That's how it is. Homer understood that we are not alone in the pursuit of our destiny. If we align ourselves with life, life's natural forces will work in our direction.

Speaking of his time in the woods surrounding Walden Pond, Thoreau said in *Walden*, "I learned this, at least, by my experiment: that if one advances confidently in the direction of his dreams, and endeavors to live the life which he has imagined, he will meet with a success unexpected in common hours." Surely he knew that when it comes to personal success there is more operating than the strength of personal will. Please do not feel alone when in actuality all of life, even when unseen, is standing with you and urging you on.

5. Because of the nature of my work, I have had the good fortune of sharing in the life transitions of many of my patients. When they have passed through the storm and renewed their lives, they often thank me for my presence and encouragement, never realizing how much their own effort, courage, and passion helped move me forward in life. I always respond in the same way: "What I have given to you is the only way that I can thank those who have given to me. Some day someone you know will be called to a transition. They will face the same fears and the same unknown as you did. Whatever help you feel that I have given to you, please pass it on to someone else who has the courage, as did you, to awaken their life." In Albert Schweitzer's words in *The Teaching of Reverence for Life,* "One must pay a price for all these boons. What one owes in return is a special responsibility for other people's lives." In our time, we call that "paying it forward."

EXERCISE #5: SHAPE SHIFTING

Letting go of the past, moving through the unknown, and gaining pivotal insights and understandings prepares us for the return to daily life. The preceding meditative practices establish a foundation for our authentic self to emerge and assert itself in daily life.

It is important to continue the basic exercises described in this book. Continuous training of the mind overcomes uncontrollable mind chatter, stabilizes the mind's natural stillness, and provides a continuous source of inner peace, contentment, and knowledge. The success of meditation and mind training is dependent on the ability to maintain mental stability and clarity. So your major practice throughout your transition and after is calming the mind and resting in stillness.

The Practice

Guided Imagery: Life as It Was

You will now do a guided-imagery meditation to explore the character of your reentry into daily life. Begin with your usual meditation practice—calming the mind and resting in stillness. Maintain your practice in this manner until establishing mental stability. This is characterized by clarity (remember the metaphor of the aquarium), non-distraction (thoughts and feelings may arise but they come and go without causing distraction), and a sense of presence and stillness. If you are unable to attain a state of inner calm, proceed with the exercise as described below.

Imagine yourself in a small private movie theater. You are looking at a blank screen. Resting quietly as an impartial observer, somewhat like a neutral journalist, allow a movie to appear that reflects your life as it was prior to your transitional process. Notice the roles you played, the character of your relationships and work, the patterns reflected in your life, the activity of your mind, and the rhythm and pace of your life. Carefully observe the flow of your life, as it once was. When you have let this movie play to its end, repeat it once more, observing the subtleties of your previous lifestyle. When completed, let the screen return to its blank state, and reflect on your observations.

Guided Imagery: A Revitalized Life

Now allow a second movie to unfold on the screen. Simply put forth the intention to see how your life will form itself in the months and years ahead. Once again, as a neutral observer, notice the roles you will step into, the character of your relationships and work, the shifting values that will guide your life, and its rhythm and pace. Be aware of the shifts in your energy level as well as other subtle changes. When you have let this movie play to its end, repeat it once more, observing the subtleties of your emerging new approach to life. When completed, let the screen return to its blank state and reflect on your observations.

Conclude this guided meditation by returning to your regular meditation practice, resting in stillness until the session is completed. You may wish to write some notes regarding your observations.

Integrating Practice into Daily Life

For your daily life practice, I suggest that you focus on work. Irrespective of the nature of your work, transform it into practice. Bring it onto the path to a larger life. At times, work can be difficult and frustrating; at other times, it can be joyful and satisfying. Whichever it may be in the moment, maintain mental calm, loving-kindness toward all whom you encounter, and convert difficulties into teaching circumstances. Take "5-minute meditative breaks," spontaneous flashbacks that access the memory of mental stillness, bring presence and mindful listening into all your interactions, and inquire as to what you can learn from difficulties and adversities.

If you hold an intention to "use" work as a teaching and practice, and remain mindful and practice these three suggestions, you can learn to transform your experience of work, using it as a daily practice. It is not as much the character of work that determines its role in your movement toward a larger life, but rather how you relate to it that transforms your experience. Add this practice to your other daily practices. Progressively, you are transforming all of daily life into practice. Said another way, your life becomes your practice and your practice becomes your life.

Chapter 7

STAGE SIX:
The Gold

There was never any more inception that there is now,

Nor any more youth or age than there is now;

And will never be any more perfection than there is now,

Nor any more heaven or hell that there is now.

—WALT WHITMAN, FROM *LEAVES OF GRASS*

The reward for the completion of a heroic journey is the return home to who and what we are. Stripped of old fears, limitations, illusions, and fantasies, we can engage life with the aliveness and freshness of an early spring morning. The capacity and effort to self-transform is a mark of the nobility of human life. And, finally, we can begin to write the first bare line of a revitalized life of authenticity and freedom.

The gold, the sun, the boon, wisdom, freedom, and *enlightenment* are words we use to express what awaits those who dare to risk all for the sole purpose of taking the adventure that leads to authentic selfhood and wholeness. Thoreau tells us that those who take the journey " . . . will live with the license of a higher order of beings." What is it that is given, permitted, and licensed to those who choose a life of consciousness? We are allowed to experience a unique and enduring *happiness, peace, wisdom, love, freedom, and health* that are innate to our humanity, already and always present within us, yet revealed and accessible only to those who have explored the depths and expanse of their lives.

The attainment of these qualities is a process, which progresses in tandem with inner development. At first we may have brief glimpses. These are important. However brief, that parting of the clouds shows us the essence of our being and the full potential of our humanity. It is not something we will forget, even in our darkest hours. Be patient with these early and brief glimpses. Be gentle. Once we've seen our full possibility, we have both a clear sense of our direction and a compelling experience that inspires and motivates our forward movement. In time, these small islands of possibility expand and coalesce. That's the gift of the journey of transition and transformation.

Happiness Without a Cause

The *happiness and joy* I am speaking of is quite different from the experience of pleasure. Pleasure arises when our desires, cravings, and fantasies are gratified in the immediate moment. For that moment, we may experience a "false happiness." Why is it false? It is false because pleasure is transient and perishable, eventually leading to an increasing desire for the object of pleasure, craving, attachment, loss, and suffering. Everything external is impermanent and will eventually change. That is why all outer derived pleasure is destined to be lost. Small moments of pleasure are gained at the cost of future disappointment and distress.

Authentic happiness comes from the inside rather than the outside. It is always accessible and nonperishable. It arises when we live in accordance with our nature—when we feel at one with ourselves and with life. It requires nothing outside of our self—neither a person, nor an experience or material object. Because it is not dependent on an outer circumstance, it is immune to the adversities of human life.

As long as we maintain contact with our natural self, inner

happiness is sustained and enduring. Because clouds obscure the sun does not mean the sun is not present. It is the same with inner happiness. It is ever present. It cannot be lost. It can only be forgotten. It's self-existent happiness. It exists by virtue of its own power. It is also called happiness without a reason, or happiness without a cause.

The Peace That Surpasses Understanding

The *peace* that I am speaking of is not the same as relaxation. Relaxation is a transient reduction in mental and physiological stress. When we say we are "really relaxed," what we generally mean is that we are experiencing our lowest level of stress. Relaxation can be enhanced through a variety of techniques, including biofeedback, massage, yoga, exercise, breathing techniques, meditation, visual imagery, and hypnosis. But in every instance, it's transient. We will reexperience our unresolved stress as soon as the temporary effects of the technique dissipate.

As with authentic happiness, serenity is a natural quality of our inner life. We discover its presence in the natural resting place of the mind. When our mind slows down, restlessness dissipates, and our cognitive mind takes a vacation, we experience our natural state of well-being, and that's peace.

With time and effort, this natural serenity becomes our norm, and the days of stress and distress become a faint memory. That transformation takes time and patience and arrives in increments, but it's the certain gift of a well-used human life.

Not dependent on methods or other outer manipulations, this inner peace is hardy, resilient, and immune to the complexities of our outer life. It has been called "the peace that surpasses understanding." Similarly to the happiness described above, it is referred to as self-existent peace, or peace without a reason or cause. When we rest in the center of our being, there it is—where it has always been.

Wisdom

There are three different types of knowledge. *Informational or descriptive knowledge* provides us with a description of the phenomenon of day-to-day existence. A car manual, cookbook, and architectural diagrams are examples of descriptive knowledge. *Intellectual knowledge* delves deeper. It analyzes conventional phenomenon to provide a deeper understanding of their mechanics and structure. Science and philosophy are examples of intellectual knowledge. The *insight and wisdom* gained through traversing life's transitions is quite different from these important, yet ordinary, forms of knowledge.

Wisdom comes from direct experience rather than intellectual inquiry. For example, I can describe to you the taste of a mango, or, through scientific analysis, delve into the biologic characteristics of the taste and taste receptors. That is cognitive knowledge, the first two forms of knowledge. But only when you taste a mango, will you actually *know* the taste of the mango, as the immediate result of your *direct personal experience.* In the same way, wisdom derived through the experience of conscious living is knowledge about life that is firsthand, precise, and derived solely from direct experience.

As we move through our life transitions, we gain knowledge by being present to life as it happens in the moment. We learn the truth of impermanence by directly experiencing it in the in-between time. We learn not to fear transient emotions and feelings by moving through them as they arise. We learn the difference between conditioned listening and true listening by practicing listening with an open mind and heart. We learn about the present moment by being forced to live in it. We gain confidence in our inner self by resting in our authentic self and knowing its invincible strength. In time these insights and wisdom grow and expand. We gain a full understanding of mind, self, other, and life. And, in that, lies our freedom to simply be.

Love and Compassion

Love and compassion similarly arise from direct experience. As we grow our inner life, we gain an accurate understanding of the underlying causes of suffering. We know how habitual patterns and perceptions lead to automatic living, with all if its misunderstandings, inner strife, and stress. We also learn that suffering which comes from automatic living can come to an end. We realize that there is so much unnecessary and unconscious suffering.

We wish that others were able to break through their confusion and blindness. We know others want to be free of suffering as much as we wish that for our self. What we want for our self, we want for others as well. That is the simple definition of compassion—to wish that others, all others, be free of suffering and the causes of suffering. An authentic, universal, and unbiased compassion naturally arises as a direct result of our personal journey. Its basis is our wise understanding of the causes of suffering and its solution.

Authentic love is the desire for others, all others, to experience an enduring and stable happiness. We have discovered through our own experience that happiness is a natural quality of our authentic self. We know it is progressively revealed to us as we dislodge the obscuring layers of our false self. We know this because we have experienced it though personal effort. We know it is present in everyone else as well. As a natural result, there arises within us a spontaneous desire that others experience the same happiness. That heartfelt desire that all individuals experience authentic happiness is love—simple, clear, and free of emotional drama.

Authentic love and compassion arise from our journey of conscious living. They are not made up by a conceptual mind that intellectually wants everyone to be happy and free of suffering. They are not mental in character. They do no result from any effort. The mother who instantaneously jumps into the water to rescue her drowning child does not think about love and compassion. She is love and compassion. Her actions are natural. They spontaneously arise, bypassing the thought process.

We've each experienced moments of natural love and compassion—a self-existent love and compassion that has no reason and no cause. As we continue to evolve our life, these experiences will become more natural and ever-present. We will know from direct experience that authentic love and compassion are natural fruits of inner development. They are not something we create.

Creativity

Creativity is originality of expression. It is a quality that can be brought to any life endeavor. However, what we usually consider to be creative is not at all original. It is a reconfiguration of ideas stored in memory that emerge in a way that may appear novel, but is grounded in previous life experience. Yes, the reconfiguration may expand our way of using past experience, but it lacks the freshness, innovation, and power of authentic creativity.

Something new cannot come from something old. Authentic creativity cannot emerge from the cognitive mind—the storage facility for previous life experience. It can only arise from the mind that has stilled cognition. The openness and spaciousness of the still mind is neither influenced nor distracted by our usual mind chatter. Creativity occurs in the still space that is free of the past and available to experience novelty. In that gap, the creative impulse and vision spontaneously arises. Just think of how your most important "aha" moments appeared. You might have to look carefully. It is likely that for a moment your thinking mind stopped, and in that gap, you experienced your "aha" experience. That is how creative people describe the process.

Creativity does not have to be a serendipitous event. We don't have to wait until that sudden gap appears and pray that a creative moment arises. The time of transition has taught us, or perhaps forced us, to live in the gap. We have learned to live in the in-between time and wait, patiently wait until clarity and vision arise naturally.

We can intentionally cultivate this inner stillness through meditative practices. The more capable we become of creating and living in a natural, clear, and open awareness, the more we are able to create the conditions and circumstances that are the fertile soil for authentic creativity. Authentic creativity results from cultivating the skills of a life transition.

Boundless Freedom

The boundless freedom we discover transcends economic and political freedom. *It's a freedom to be.* It's the freedom to live authentically and spontaneously with consciousness and heart. It arises as we're progressively released from the limiting and contracting influences of a false self and our habitual patterns of perception and reaction. Then we are able, for the first time, to live free of the known, free of the past, and experience life fully in the present *as it is.* The basis of boundless freedom is a shift from automatic living to conscious living. It naturally arises from this center of our being. It is vital, dynamic, and joyful.

Authentic happiness, enduring peace, insight and wisdom, love and compassion, and boundless freedom are not mere words or experiences that we "fall" into on a fortunate day. They are gifts that come with growing our human life, gifts we've obscured by automatic living. When we live consciously, in accord with our nature, these human capacities are revealed in their full luminosity—a human/divine treasure that was never really lost. We cannot grasp or create these human qualities. They are the results of a well-lived life.

These gifts of transition and conscious living are available to each of us. First we are offered glimpses of our true nature and its qualities. This inspires us to go further on our path of inner development. These islands of experience slowly coalesce into larger land masses, and in time, what was once a glimpse progressively becomes our life. One morning we wake up and realize we have changed, really changed. It feels good. It feels right. It feels who and what we are. Then, with tears, comes gratitude.

The goal of the alchemical procedure was the production of the golden metal. As the last chapters of the history of alchemy were being recorded, it was increasingly apparent to the alchemists that the transformation they sought with such great dedication was occurring. However, it was not occurring in their flasks, but rather, it was occurring in themselves. As it turned out, the end result of their 1,700-year effort, the *opus alchemicum,* was self-knowledge, the psychological and spiritual gold.

The deepest passion of the Western mind, according to Richard Tarnas in his book *The Passion of the Western Mind,* is for the mind to realize itself, to forge its own autonomy, and to reunite with the ground of its being. To this end, the ancient alchemists are joined by philosophers, religious figures, artists, modern-day scientists, and you and me. We are all searching for the same gold—selfhood and wholeness.

At the darkest moments of the in-between time, this may seem far away, yet it is always near, much nearer than you imagine. All we need to do is to stay with our experience and live our transitions to their end. When the proper ripening has occurred, selfhood and wholeness will naturally and effortlessly reveal themselves. And, finally, we will bring the divine wisdom achieved at the depths into the human act of living life.

HEART ADVICE FROM A FELLOW TRAVELER

1. The six stages of a life transition—the *Call,* the *Departure,* the *In-Between Time,* the *Lessons Learned,* the *Return,* and the

Gold—have been well known throughout the ages. Their unfolding varied in character according to culture and custom. In modern times, we have lost the support and guidance they offer. I felt this in my first major transition. There was little guidance to be found. It was like falling into an abyss without a way out.

Fortunately, I did find guidance from wise teachers. This support was of critical importance. It gave me assurance that I wasn't "crazy" or isolated. An awareness of the stages of transition was like having a map. You know the starting point, the end point, and the steps in between. There is less likelihood of being lost and advanced notice about the challenges of each stage. This lends an important confidence and faith that assures that you have made the right choice, taken the right journey, and that its end, the dawning of a new light, will come in time.

As mentioned previously, reading the great stories of transition and transformation were of great value to me. Not only did I learn about the firsthand process of others, but I also learned about the fruits of transition discussed in this chapter. The path to be taken and the inevitable emergence of these noble human qualities and capacities are consistent throughout literature and healing traditions. In the darkest of nights, that assured me that staying the course would lead to the great treasures of human life. That knowledge was the light that kept me going.

2. You are not "wasting" time by taking the time to live your life transition. Time is wasted when we continue to live automatically. Time is wasted when we live on the surface of relationships rather that experience the full majesty of connection and intimacy. Time is wasted when we satisfy our self with the instant gratification of superficial pleasures. Time is wasted when we instinctively live a self-serving life rather than a life of selfless service. Time is wasted when we live a life of contraction rather than expansion. That is how we waste time. The time taken for

transition is an extraordinary investment in life. Do not wait until the end of life to discover who and what you are.

3. When you undertake the challenge of a life transition, you may feel different from some of your friends. Their lives may seem to be moving forward with new relationships, promotions at work, acquired possessions, and endless activities and pleasures. I know that feeling. Look around. We live in a culture that has given rise to epidemics of stress and posttraumatic stress, mental distress of all sorts, addiction, mood disorders, unstable relationships, premature disease, suicide, and attention deficit disorders, to mention a few. It is difficult to take "normal" for healthy. It is incorrect to believe that anyone escapes the consequences of an unawakened life. They don't. To follow the ways of modern life, rather than the urgings of your soul, is the difference between falling into these epidemics or gaining the fullness of human life and health.

Look at the great beings that you know. Read their stories. Their journey is not one of common ways. They have taken the road less traveled. They have met life's challenges with intention, consciousness, and spirit. They have traversed those difficult moments as a hero. Take comfort in your inner journey. It follows the path of those before you who have also followed the inner call. Their lives have been of immeasurable benefit to humankind.

4. It is difficult to move through a major life transition without a mentor. You wouldn't think of learning a language or skill without a teacher. It is no different learning about your life. There are problems and obstacles that may occur, particularly difficult moments when faith is dimmed, wrong turns along the way, and other challenging moments. When these occur, support and advice from a wise mentor is quite helpful.

It is important to choose a mentor carefully. There are many coaches and counselors. If they are inexperienced and have not walked the walk, they are not for you. Avoid individuals with new "methods" or "quick" approaches. Look for wisdom, experience, patience, kindness, a life consciously lived, a teacher who is an ongoing student of life. Use your judgment and discernment. And, if your first choice is not right, let it go and try again. Mentors are special people. Find the one who's right for you.

EXERCISE #6: OPENING THE HEART

We have come a distance in our effort to create a healthy human life. That alone is a great accomplishment for any individual at any time in history. The central process has been to move beyond outdated and inauthentic habitual patterns of perception and reaction toward a way of being that is easefully and effortlessly natural. A central tool in this process has been the use of meditation. First, we calm the overactive mind, then we gain an understanding of our life and life itself, and finally we gain access to the higher qualities of human life. That is a patient and progressive process.

In the Eastern traditions there is often a single word for mind and heart. The observation made is that a clear, open, and wise mind and heart arise together. When we cultivate our inner life as an important aid to a life transition, we simultaneously cultivate heart. When we cultivate our heart we are simultaneously cultivating a clear and still mind. As we increasingly live from our authentic self, our heart softens and defensiveness and protectiveness drop away. In this last exercise, you will work directly on opening the heart and stilling the mind with a very powerful traditional practice called "giving and taking."

The Practice

Giving and Taking with a Loved One

As before, begin this practice by calming the mind and progressing to a natural stillness. You don't need a perfectly clear mind. Quiet the mind as best as you can, and when your mind is sufficiently stable, you can proceed with the "giving and taking" aspect of the practice.

Create a mental image of an individual in your life whom you hold with love and care. Place this image in front of your visual field. Feel the love and care as it radiates in both directions.

Begin with your out-breathe. Riding the out-breath toward the other individual is the aspiration that your loved one experiences the natural and enduring happiness that is found within each of us. You know this from your own inner journey, and now you wish it for your loved one. In fact, you drop into the well of your own well-being and give from it to the other. For a few minutes practice giving out this aspiration to your loved one on each out-breathe—that they have happiness and well-being. Feel your heart open. Feel the connection. Feel that authentic wish that your loved one discover this universal and hardy sense of well-being.

Next, begin working with the in-breath. We know that suffering results from an inauthentic life—from outdated habits, perceptions, and reactions that disturb body, mind, and speech. We know the cause of this is an absence of our authentic self. We know that it is possible to progressively rejoin our authentic self and bring an end to mental distress and suffering. Therefore, with each in-breath, you aspire to free your loved one of the causes of self-created mental suffering.

Attach inner well-being to the out-breath and send it out to your loved one. Attach to the in-breath the aspiration that your loved one be free of suffering and the causes of suffering. Continue this practice for five minutes.

Giving and Taking with a Stranger
Next, drop the image of your loved one and replace it with the image of a stranger. It could be a random person in a movie theater, on a bus, or so on. Your feelings will be neutral toward this unknown individual. Begin the same "giving and taking" exercise with this stranger. Continue for five minutes. Observe your heart. Observe your experience with this unknown other.

Giving and Taking with a Challenging Individual
Next, move toward the most difficult aspect of this practice, giving and taking with someone you dislike or consider difficult. Remember, true love and compassion have an unbiased quality to them. You are not justifying the personality or behavior of this individual, but just relating to his or her core of humanity.

We understand the ignorance and confusion that underlies mental distress and destructive behavior. We understand that challenging individuals are compelled by past experience. Surely we wish that all individuals could eliminate the causes of suffering that are the basis of destructive behavior. Surely we wish that even these individuals could discover the ever-present treasures of goodness and gentleness. With this in mind, begin to practice with the image of this individual. You are working with a full heart and desire to open this individual to the center of his or her being. Remember, you are focused on the basic humanity of this individual, not on his or her disturbed outer self. Continue this practice for five minutes.

Giving and Taking as a Universal Experience
Finally, let this image go and imagine yourself on a hilltop, overlooking and facing a vast and seemingly endless field. In front of you are all of your loved ones, and behind are all other beings. With this full array of humanity, begin the giving and taking practice, including everyone. Continue this practice for five min-

utes. At the conclusion, let this image fade away, remaining in your heart.

Giving and Taking with Yourself

Now, let this and all other images dissolve, and return to an inner stillness. Give yourself the well-being that is in your natural resting place. This well-being will bring you peace and ease and remove emotional afflictions, stress, and distress. This is an important aspect of self-compassion and self-care. Rest in stillness and basic well-being for the concluding five minutes of your practice.

Of course, we can neither give true happiness to others nor remove their causes of suffering. But this exercise, your intention and aspiration to do so, opens your heart, diminishes the tenacity of your self-cherishing ego, and brings you into greater understanding and harmony with others. This is an essential component of creating a healthy human life.

Integrating Practice into Daily Life

As a final daily practice, I would like you to spend a few minutes here and there during the day practicing giving and taking with others in your daily life. This is your way of becoming a healer, your way of opening your heart, your way of clearing your mind. It all works together—healthy heart and healthy mind equals a healthy life.

If you maintain and mature your normal sitting practice and day-to-day practice, you will greatly facilitate the successful movement through your life transition and cultivate the skills that will assure a hardy, healthy human life.

Chapter 8

A Healthy Human Life
and Beyond

I shall be telling this with a sigh
Somewhere ages and ages hence:
Two roads diverged in a wood, and I –
I took the one less travelled by,
And that has made all the difference.

—ROBERT FROST, "THE ROAD NOT TAKEN"

The wise ones tell us that we must take our time in the quest for personal authenticity and human flourishing. We must take the path that goes through adversity and challenge, through the varied experiences of human life. It is in that crucible of life that we are fully prepared to see and experience an intimate knowledge of life.

But it is not any path that will take us in this direction. It is the path that walks into and navigates our life transitions with grace, skill, intent, and faith. It is the path less traveled through the "hardships" of life that takes us toward a healthy human life and opens the door to what lies beyond. What lies beyond can hardly be spoken of with accuracy. It remains an open question, an open and evolving possibility. It is an unfolding experience and exploration that embraces and transcends day-to-day life.

The key element is conscious evolution that's akin to biological evolution. As we progressively grow in consciousness through our transitions, we progressively touch the edges of human

potential where we discover the most refined capacities and qualities of human life. Although we cannot bring it about by will,
when we establish favorable conditions, we will one day unexpectedly wake up and experience the magnificence of life. We
will then know with certainty the fulfillment of our humanity
and our role in the evolution of human life.

There are three preliminaries that are traditionally the
entranceway to this special realm of existence. They are surrender,
devotion, and unity consciousness. Let's look at each of these.

Surrender

If we lived full time in our night dreams, we would never know
the day-to-day world of ordinary wakefulness. But, each morning
upon arising, we renounce our dream world as unreal, as the
product of our imagination. We do not renounce that we've had
a dream. If fact, the dream may contain useful information that
reveals our unconscious life. But rather, we let go of the belief,
held in the dream state, that the dream is real—real and solid
people and experiences.

As difficult and strange as it may seem, much the same is
required as we move from ordinary experience to the peaks of
human existence. We are required to let go of—that is, surrender—the belief that day-to-day experience is a solid, unchanging,
fixed reality. That comes only with the realization that all things
are ever-changing according to momentary causes, conditions,
and circumstances. A rainbow may appear solid and substantial
to us, but we know it only exists by virtue of the aggregation of
the factors of light, moisture, refraction, diffraction, our visual
apparatus, and our consciousness, which together allow the experience of this transient appearance.

When we realize that our day-to-day world is an ever-changing landscape, we are closer to understanding the true nature of

our life. As a result, our day-to-day life begins to soften and flow. We no longer attach to, nor react to, life as solid and permanent. Thus, we no longer look toward any one experience or person with the illusionary belief that it or they will reliably and forever fulfill our desire for enduring happiness, peace, and authenticity.

The difficulty here is that we must turn inward to gain that realization. Letting go of our overinvestment in the outer world as a source of enduring peace and happiness is a preliminary to the sustained inward turn that is required to go further. It is important to note that we are not turning away from our outer life. We are turning away from a false belief in what outer life can deliver, and turning toward an inner life for what it *can* deliver— a deeper and more enduring experience.

In summary, to gain a healthy human life and then move beyond to the pinnacle of human achievement, there must be a strong longing that drives us further inward with passion. That's difficult to accomplish when we have not yet seen and known the transcendent treasures of spiritual life. It's a poignant process, perhaps a sense of loss, as is any letting go of long-held beliefs and behaviors.

We know we're ready when our craving for knowledge, authenticity, and the fullness of life moves through every cell of our body. Our whole being wants to experience the essence and guts of life and cares less and less for the usual trappings of ordinary existence. Spiritual wealth is seen as the gold. The material and social rewards of ordinary life are seen as mere pacifiers. When that thirst drives our life, then we are ready for the journey beyond.

Devotion

"Devotion" is an unusual word to use in the West. Although we don't usually think about it, when we carefully examine our life, we'll likely discover that we are devoted. We are devoted to pro-

tecting, defending, securing, and embellishing our sense of self—
the territory of the "I." As long as we live life focused on our self,
there is no possibility of moving beyond. The ego and all of its
needs, noise, manipulations, and restless energy does not allow
for the sustained clarity and stillness that opens the door to a
transcendent life.

Immersed in the business of the ego, we cannot know or see
beyond its desires and obscurations. Moving beyond requires that
we place the desire for wisdom, peace, authentic happiness, compassion, and truth at the center of our life. These qualities, which
together are our true nature, must be our source of devotion.

To be devoted to our full human development is a noble
endeavor. However, it is not easy. That is not the way we have
been raised. It is not supported by culture. It's often not understood by loved ones, family, and friends. There are no medals or
blue ribbons. We may feel different from others. We may feel
alone. Yet, it is the unique path, told over and over, to the fulfillment of our humanity,

Devotion to the inner life must be accompanied by an ardor
and zeal. If not, daily life concerns will always come first. Once
again, this does not mean we give up daily life or its activities and
responsibilities. We carry out our duties with grace and elegance
as we infuse them with inner light. Our priority and energy, however, go toward opening our spiritual life through study, reflection, practice, and selfless service. Devotion to exploring the far
reaches of life is the second preliminary for the journey beyond.

Unity Consciousness

There are three levels of awareness/consciousness. The first level
is moment-to-moment experience. This can be referred to as
mindful living in contrast to automatic living. That requires
training attention, concentration, and mindfulness. Without

these qualities, our mind is overtaken by restless mental activity, leaving little space for an actual moment-to-moment awareness. Mind training and meditation begin with calming the mind. It is the basis of the higher forms of awareness.

The second level is recognition of the essential nature of mind—its stillness, clarity, and spaciousness. As the mind achieves a progressive state of stillness, it becomes possible to experience its natural resting place free of incessant activity. Like the silt settling in water, the mind's expansiveness and clarity become self-evident. Of course, like the ever-present sun obscured and rendered invisible by clouds, the natural stillness, peace, and clarity of the mind cannot be seen until the obscuring mental activity is calmed. When this occurs, there is the slow and natural appearance of an open awareness undisturbed by random movements of the mind.

This level of awareness allows one to see what is, as is, without the filtering and shaping of the cognitive mind with its habitual and conditioned patterns of perception. This leads to insights regarding mind and life that grow into a life-enhancing wisdom. A still, clear, and bare awareness is the second level of awareness. It is a great achievement and in itself is sufficient for a healthy human life.

The pinnacle and third level of awareness is called unity consciousness. This third level of awareness takes one beyond the duality of day-to-day life, beyond "I and It," "I and Other," and "Subject and Object." Those who have achieved this level of experience live in a seamless oneness and unity with all of life. They may participate in all of the complexities of day-to-day life, but they do not live in that complexity. They are in the world but not of it.

They know the very human dualistic experience of ordinary life and can be fully in it. Yet, they also know it is but an expression of a far deeper unity that is beyond "this and that." We have all had moments of unity consciousness, but to achieve that as the core of one's life is remarkable. This third level of consciousness, unity consciousness, is what characterizes the mystic and his or her profound knowledge of universal oneness.

I would like to say that I have had some achievement of the preliminaries of letting go, devotion, and higher levels of awareness/consciousness. I have not. Here and there I may have been fortunate to have a brief taste and glimpse, but I claim no more than that. I am merely repeating the words and advice of others. That is how I have attempted to introduce this refined pinnacle of human existence. So at least we can see the entire picture of the evolution of human consciousness that can be achieved through living our transitions, even if our lifetime is not destined to go to that far end.

Let's now take a brief overview of some of the qualities and capacities that arise as we progressively master these three preliminaries.

Non-Locality

Our day-to-day life is lived as a local affair guided by sensory perceptions and mental conceptions. Like Newtonian physics, this is a physical and material world of cause and effect. The common perspective is that consciousness is a product of brain functioning and is limited to local biological events. As a result of sufficient biological development, human consciousness is said to emerge. Brain and consciousness are considered one and the same.

It would be difficult to deny our own experience. Consciousness, as we ordinarily experience it, appears to be greatly affected by brain trauma, altered brain physiology, and ceases at death. The great traditions do not deny the strong relationship between consciousness and the brain, but they assert that there is an aspect of consciousness that is universal, permeates all of life, and is not based on brain function. Surely we cannot understand this through usual logic.

But logic is not what is used to experience this transcendent consciousness. For that we need to look to the field of inquiry called *phenomenology*. Phenomenology refers to the direct personal experience of consciousness, which arises from meditative absorption. In this state of clarity consciousness can see itself. It is self-revealing in all its subtleties. It is in that manner that spiritual teachers know and teach the non-local aspect of consciousness.

They tell us that they experience an expansive, universal, pervasive awareness, which is neither localized to the brain nor interrupted by the cycle of birth and death. It is that consciousness that allows for the unusual and incredible powers (telepathy, precognition, clairvoyance, and so on) that are reported and demonstrated by the great mystics. Their experience cuts through the notion of a localized self and localized experiences. To know it, one must advance to the final stage of meditation and commit oneself to the rigors of a life devoted to exploring the nature of reality.

Those who know do not mistake the relative day-to-day world for the universal truths that lie below. They live according to these universal principles and laws. Although their lives might seem quite ordinary, they are not. They live in the universality of awareness, the divine spirit. For them, cognition is a tool and instrument for navigating day-to-day life, but it is never mistaken as a tool to understand what lies beyond.

Love and Compassion

We are told that in the end there is only love. It is not an ordinary love and compassion. It is quite different, as it contains all of the qualities and capacities of higher levels of consciousness. It is impersonal, universal, and impartial. At this level of consciousness, the heart is open to impartially care for the needs and happiness of all—lovers, strangers, and even those we dislike.

Like the mother who jumps into the water to rescue a drowning child, the act of love and compassion is natural, fully in accord with present moment circumstances, effortless, and spontaneous. This is not an emotional response. It is authentic present moment action.

Authentic love and compassion arise from the immediate experience that another's suffering is our suffering, another's pain is our pain. We are united in a single movement of life, seamlessly whole. So it is natural and unavoidable to respond to others with compassion and love. This action is as lacking in self-conscious-ness as the perfume given forth by a flower. It's a mighty attain-ment.

Touching the Impersonal

There is nothing personal about unity consciousness. When the personal recedes, distinctions dissipate, separation comes to an end, and oneness is experienced. No longer separated by egoic walls, we are told that it is possible to experience and travel beyond self, time, and space as ordinarily perceived. I recall a stu-dent once asking a question of one of my teachers. "How," he asked, "could the great sage Milarepa fly up mountains or per-form any of the miracles attributed to him?" The teacher was silent for a moment and then answered, "When you are Milarepa, you will know."

Perhaps that is as far as we can go here. There are certain things one can only learn from direct experience. The experience of a sustained wholeness and oneness and the existence of its powerful capacities are among those things.

Moving beyond to the edges of human experience is not for all of us. It is for those who have a particular interest in the mystic life and the far reaches of the human experience. The remainder of us should be quite satisfied with the healthy human life that arises as we grow through our life transitions.

Afterword

As we gain an understanding of the transitional process, we become increasingly skilled at living life and navigating future transitions. We have found an inner core of being and developed new capacities that allow us to traverse day-to-day life while simultaneously maintaining an inner calmness. We can carefully and effectively experience the complexities of living, navigate them, and grow in wisdom and compassion.

We discover that life's challenges and adversities, when experienced deeply, can become our greatest teachers. Approached with correct understanding, knowledge, and skills, these unwanted disturbances are the basis of greatness.

We progressively become masters of two worlds—inner and outer. We are able to experience the depths of being and integrate these understandings into day-to-day life. Our life may appear quite ordinary from the outside, but it has actually become quite extraordinary. We have dared to venture into the fullness of life and, in that effort, have lost falseness and found truth, lost who we are not and found who we are, lost a fool's gold and gained true gold.

This is not a journey for the faint hearted. It requires courage, faith, and vision. Yet, when you surrender to this journey, special helpers arise along the way. You are never alone. You are part of an evolutionary journey whose aim is a larger and healthier life for all living beings.

Thus, your story is part of a larger story. Your breakthrough is part of a larger breakthrough. Your discovery of personal gold is an important link in the movement toward a greater humanity. Your transition is a noble and sacred act, a gift to life.

Working With Elliott

Personal Mentoring

Each of us will face one or more major transitions in our lifetime. As discussed in this book, the outcome will depend upon the understanding and skills we bring to this process. Transitions can be seen as difficult, challenging, and unwanted, or they can be sources of personal growth, new opportunities, and a larger and more fulfilled life.

It is difficult to navigate a life transition by oneself or even with the best-intentioned friends. We have to avail ourselves of skilled guidance and support. That is how it has been for me in my life. Skilled mentors smooth the way and assure a successful outcome.

Mentorship is a special relationship—a unique trusted friendship in which individuals work together, through times of challenge and times of ease, to unfold a living experience that is authentic, full, intimate, and meaningful in body, mind, and spirit.

I currently offer mentoring and coaching services to a small number of individuals. This is a serious commitment that calls upon my years of experience as a physician, a meditation teacher, and a heartfelt fellow traveler on the road to a fulfilled life. To learn more about these services please refer to the "Working with Elliott" section on my website: www.elliottdacher.org.

Suggested Readings

The Transitional Process

Aware, Awake, Alive by Elliott Dacher

I recommend my previous book as a primer on meditation. Meditation is an invaluable companion before, during, and after a life transition. This book and the accompanying practice CD guides the reader through the development of a time-tested meditation practice.

When Things Fall Apart: Heart Advice for Difficult Times
by Pema Chödrön

Pema Chödrön has a unique gift in presenting, in a sophisticated yet practical manner, the issues related to a life transition. If you find her book helpful, I suggest further readings of her books.

Transitions: Making Sense of Life's Changes by William Bridges

This is a practical guide to life transitions that will complement the guidance given in this book.

The Alchemist by Paul Coelho

A sweet and instructive novel that follows the journey that returns us in T.S. Eliot's words "to the place from which we started." It is helpful to read inspirational books such as this.

Letters to a Young Poet by **Rainer Maria Rilke**

Rilke speaks through letters to the aspirations of a young poet he has never met. There is wise and timeless advice for all of us as we engage the journey toward a larger life.

Man's Search for Meaning by **Viktor Frankl**

How is it that when some are confronted with great adversity they prosper and grow, while others fall into despair? Speaking from his experience in a concentration camp, Frankl articulates an answer to this question, which has meaning for all of us as we face the more mundane challenges of day-to-day life.

Modern Man in Search of a Soul by **C.G. Jung**

In this book, Jung brings to his rich and timeless vision that is directly relevant to our search for a larger life of greater authenticity.

The Hero With a Thousand Faces by **Joseph Campbell**

It would not be possible to leave this book out of a resource guide to life transitions. Building on the work of psychologist C.G. Jung and has extensive knowledge as a mythologist, Campbell offers a multicultural survey of the universal process of life transitions. Consider this book only if your wish to explore this material in the context of complex mythological themes.

Freedom From the Known by **Jiddu Krishnamurti**

In this seminar work, Krishnamurti forces us to confront the deeply conditioned personal and cultural habits and patterns that define and control our lives. This is a wonderful read that I would reserve for the philosophical-minded reader.

The Great Stories

As mentioned throughout this book, my transitions have been inspired by the great journeys recorded in literature. Here is a sampling:

Siddhartha by Hermann Hesse

Mount Analogue by René Daumal

The Story of Odysseus by Homer

The Oedipus Cycle by Sophocles

She: Understanding Feminine Psychology by Robert Johnson

He: Understanding Masculine Psychology by Robert Johnson

Retreat Facilities

Insight Meditation Society
Pleasant Street
Barre, Massachusetts 01001

Spirit Rock Center
P.O. Box 909
Woodacre, California 94973

Both of these organizations offer intensive mindfulness meditation retreats. These retreats are an opportunity for intensive study under the guidance of skilled teachers. They are highly recommended for both beginners and advanced students.

58135112R00085

Made in the USA
Charleston, SC
01 July 2016